GREAT
ENGLISH
GARDENS

GREAT ENGLISH GARDENS

ANDREW LAWSON & JANE TAYLOR

WEIDENFELD & NICOLSON · LONDON

CONTENTS

Photographer's note. I am immensely grateful to the garden-owners, gardeners and designers who have welcomed me to their gardens. Their hospitality has often extended to breakfasts, lunches and a comfortable room for the night. Their many kindnesses, and the beauty of the gardens, have made me appreciate how privileged is the life of a garden photographer. I hope that just some of my gratitude and pleasure comes across in the pictures. *A.L.*

First published in Great Britain in 1996 by George Weidenfeld & Nicolson Ltd
The Orion Publishing Group
Orion House
5 Upper St Martin's Lane
London WC2H 9EA

ISBN 0 297 83622 6

A CIP catalogue record for this book is available from the British Library.

Designed by Harry Green

Printed and bound in Italy

ENDPAPERS:
Soft harmonies at Sticky Wicket, Dorset, with purple sage and violas, and the toothed leaves of *Dendranthema pacificum*.
PAGE 1:
Classic spring bedding at Garsington Manor, Oxfordshire: forget-me-nots and yellow, lily-flowered *Tulipa* 'Westpoint'
PAGE 2:
A view across the pool garden at Hidcote Manor, Gloucestershire, with topiary and Hidcote's well-known tapestry hedge beyond.
PAGE 3:
Roses and delphiniums, the essence of an English garden in summer, at Haddon Hall, Derbyshire.
RIGHT:
A gem of a town garden, designed by Anthony Noel, in Fulham, west London.

MAJOR TWENTIETH-CENTURY INFLUENCES

S IR EDWIN LUTYENS CAPTURED THE SPIRIT OF THE EDWARDIAN AGE IN ENGLAND, THE LAST GASP OF THE GRACIOUS LIFE THAT WAS TO BE SO DRAMATICALLY ENDED WITH THE OUTBREAK OF THE GREAT WAR IN 1914. THE NOSTALGIC MEMORIES OF GOLDEN AFTERNOONS LINGER ON IN THIS VIEW OF THE GARDENS AT HESTERCOMBE, SOMERSET, DESIGNED BY LUTYENS AND FEATURING HIS HALLMARKS: THE STONE-LINED RILL, OR NARROW WATER COURSE; THE FLIGHT OF STONE STEPS; AND THE MASSIVE PERGOLA, ITS ALTERNATING ROUND AND SQUARE PILLARS, COMPOSED OF SLIVERS OF STONE, TOPPED BY OAK CROSS BEAMS, DRAPED IN ROSES AND CLEMATIS. THE JEKYLL PLANTINGS ARE ONCE AGAIN AS SHE INTENDED THEM, WITH HER HALLMARK BERGENIAS, LAVENDER, SANTOLINA, LILIES AND YUCCAS.

Any garden that both enchants at first sight and satisfies over a lifetime's loving familiarity is likely to belong to someone who knows how to balance plantsmanship and picture gardening. The gardens featured in this book range from grand estates to modest cottage plots; whatever their size, they have in common this quality of balance, and a sense of repose spiced with an element of surprise. Some of them pre-date the modern era and illustrate the influences that have marked the gardens of Britain over the centuries. The great gardens of this century – great not necessarily in size, but decidedly so in importance – show above all the influence of a handful of artist-plantsmen and women: Gertrude Jekyll, Vita Sackville-West, Lawrence Johnston.

Gertrude Jekyll's constant preoccupation was to make what she called 'beautiful pictures'. Few of her planting schemes survive in their original form, though some have been restored; but her garden plans and her books live on, and through them, in the minds of countless gardeners, the pictures she strove for and so successfully achieved.

LEFT: Twin borders in the garden at House of Pitmuies, Angus, are framed by the silvery foliage of *Pyrus salicifolia* 'Pendula', the weeping silver pear. The strong verticals of delphiniums give form to an otherwise soft, feathery planting of cloudy outlines, and the eye is drawn to the pillared gate and a tantalizing glimpse of fields and wooded slopes beyond. Miss Jekyll would surely have approved of the way in which blues and yellows are used here, with perhaps just a question-mark against the inclusion of lilac-mauve tones. She wrote 'I always find more satisfaction and facility in treating... the cool [colours] in contrasts; especially in the case of blue, which I like to use ... in distinct but not garish contrasts, as of full blue with pale yellow ...'.

ABOVE: In the influential *Gardens for Small Country Houses* (1914), written by Gertrude Jekyll and Lawrence Weaver, the authors lament the 'steady increase in the use of motor-cars' that made carriage entrances necessary. This gate at Hestercombe, however, at the top of a flight of stone steps, is of the kind known as a foot-gate, and recalls a time before the advent of the internal combustion engine.

RIGHT: Designed in 1903, Hestercombe's garden had become derelict; since 1973 it has been reclaimed. First to be restored was the Lutyens stonework in all its varied textural detail. Attention then turned to the Jekyll plantings. The hot colours and strong vertical lines of red hot pokers and mullein are here contained in a narrow border backed by a wall which has itself become part of the planting.

RIGHT: Looking down on the garden at Sissinghurst, Kent, from the vantage point of the Elizabethan tower, one can see that the firm lines of clipped hedge and wall and path, which seem so symmetrical at ground-level, have been imaginatively drawn to fit the awkwardly-shaped site. This framework lends coherence to the varied planting, while the empty rondel at the heart of the rose garden emphasizes the rich, almost overblown abundance of the rose beds themselves with their dense underplantings in a restricted palette of soft pinks and mauves. The garden wall was the back wall of one wing of the original house; a door and window have been preserved in it.

ABOVE: The famous White Garden at Sissinghurst has been much eulogized and emulated, but perhaps never surpassed. It has an ethereal magic, its white flowers and grey and silver foliage seeming all the more insubstantial for being captured within beds outlined in the strong green of clipped box. There are lilies and tobacco flowers for fragrance – both exhaling their scent most poignantly on the night air, when their whiteness gleams in the dusk. There are white poppies, white lupins, stately silver Scotch thistles and the blue-grey blades of lyme grass around the central bower of white rambler rose. Elsewhere are pungent silver santolinas and grey artemisias, and an elegantly weeping silver pear.

RIGHT: A restrained palette of colours makes for easeful harmonies, as here at Sissinghurst where shades of pink, mauve, magenta and violet in a border of shrub roses and alliums, backed by an old wall, are glimpsed through a porthole clipped in the yew hedge. Yew, given a good start in enriched soil, is not as slow to make a mature-looking hedge as impatient gardeners sometimes imagine.

When Miss Jekyll was in her middle years, towards the end of the nineteenth century, she met the young Edwin Lutyens, who was at the very start of his career as an architect. An extraordinarily creative partnership developed between them which produced over a hundred gardens. Lutyens designed for them, in characteristic style, a more or less formal setting of stone or brick work, much of which has endured (see also page 67), and Miss Jekyll provided the planting schemes.

Despite the success of the partnership between Lutyens and Gertrude Jekyll, garden-making was only a minor strand in Lutyens' remarkable career

as an architect; and the lavish use of architectural detail in the garden, typical not only of Lutyens himself but of his era, was to give way between and after the wars to a greater emphasis on plants as the structure as well as the decor of the garden. Miss Jekyll's role in this development has been immense. Even if some of her suggestions too clearly imply a large staff of head- and under-gardeners and a bothy of gardeners' boys, her writings remain uniquely influential. Her pages are filled with tempting associations of plants, tips and contrivances; and not all her designs are for borders with a concentrated season of impact demanding

LEFT: In spring, lily-of-the-valley and, beyond the low hedge, honeysuckle azaleas perfume the air in the moat walk at Sissinghurst.

ABOVE: The same view in the height of summer, with montbretia and the grand old *Dahlia* 'Bishop of Llandaff', with its metallic black-purple foliage and refulgent scarlet flowers, assertively claiming the foreground. The simplicity of soft mauve and an abundance of green, beyond the hedge, both emphasize the red in the foreground and seem to lengthen the perspective of the path that leads the eye to the twin verticals of the white statue and the distant poplar.

constant attention. She also excelled at the more relaxed style of planting which offers some cameo to hold the eye at all seasons, and knew exactly how to handle the transition from formal to informal.

Trained as an artist, she articulated in her books a theory of colour which is as relevant today as when she first put it into practice. Her flower borders of a single colour or a narrow range of harmonies have proved a lasting inspiration, not difficult to translate to today's smaller gardens.

Harder to achieve, especially in a small space, are her graded colour schemes, in which opalescent tones of grey and glaucous foliage with flowers of pure blue and white, cream and dawn pink at one end of a long border gradually yield through shades of yellow to warm and then to glowing hot oranges and reds at the midpoint, before cooling once more through pastel tints accompanied, this time, by purple and lilac flowers with glaucous and silver foliage. Working always in drifts and sweeps of harmonious colours, she achieved borders that were vibrant but never garish, and had an eye as much for form as for colour, using spiky yuccas as a bold end stop, or the leathery paddles of bergenias amid a haze of starry asters to soften the hard lines of masonry.

Miss Jekyll died in 1932. Two years earlier, Vita

LEFT: Sureness of design makes for a compelling picture, despite – or perhaps because of – the simplicity of the components. The brick path running through the Fuchsia Garden at Hidcote Manor, Gloucestershire, forms a strong axis to draw the eye past the pair of topiary birds and through the sombre yew that has been clipped into a pediment and square-topped doorway of monumental simplicity. The path is flanked by box-edged beds of uncomplicated geometric design filled with a single colour, echoing the azure of the sky. Beyond the plump birds on their massive plinths lies the Bathing Pool Garden, named for the raised, circular pool which almost fills this garden 'room' walled with yew.

ABOVE: The identical view in winter, the patterns etched now in snow and the Bathing Pool frozen, shows how gardens of this kind, with their good bones, transcend the flowery profusion of summer to satisfy the eye at all seasons. Hidcote is so firmly established in the canon of outstanding gardens that it is hard to imagine how entirely different it was from anything that had gone before, when Major Johnston first began to plant the hedges of yew or copper beech and the mixed tapestry hedges that form the walls of the different enclosures, and to devise the plantings of mixed shrubs and perennials, or – as in the Fuchsia Garden – of a single type of plant dominating one of the 'rooms'.

Sackville-West and her husband Harold Nicolson had first come to Sissinghurst Castle in Kent, and envisaged, despite the derelict buildings, the accumulated debris of centuries of heedless occupation, the all-invading weeds, what this strangely captivating place might become. The husband-and-wife partnership was scarcely less curious than that between Miss Jekyll and Lutyens; the two lived largely separate lives, but the garden united them.

Harold Nicolson's contribution was in the design; using the timeless elements of water, trees, hedges, brick and stone work and lawns, he laid out a garden with a firm geometric structure of long, formal vistas and enclosed spaces, tranquil and mysterious at the same time. But it was Vita who chose the plants, combining romantic profusion with a sure and disciplined eye for colour. The rose garden with its chaste central rondel of clipped yew and its abundance of old roses arching and tumbling over alliums and hostas and geraniums; the richly sombre purple border; the cottage garden planted entirely with sunset colours (see page 59); the orchard with its gnarled old fruit trees in which she set scented rambler roses; and above all the famous white garden (see page 12) – these have been echoed and emulated in hundreds of gardens the world over. Even those who have never been among the one hundred thousand or more visitors to Sissinghurst each year have drawn inspiration from her writings (she wrote a weekly garden column for a Sunday newspaper for years, and her best pieces have been reprinted) or from the many books in which Sissinghurst is illustrated, described, analysed, admired.

On the other side of England, in the county of Gloucestershire, lies Sissinghurst's great rival in the affections of garden visitors, Hidcote Manor. Like Sissinghurst, Hidcote is composed of a series of intimate, enclosed gardens, set on either side of the main axis; but its setting is very different, not the flat fields of Kent but the Cotswold hills. Hidcote is a garden of long vistas; the upward incline of the land draws the gaze not only to the hills, but above all to the wide arch of the open sky. Its strong, formal lines are composed of clipped yew or tapestry hedges or hornbeams on stilts. Within these, as at Sissinghurst, is an abundance of flowers and foliage,

in garden 'rooms' and borders of either a single colour – as in the red border, a potent visual and emotional experience at the height of its season (see page 18) – or of a simple, harmonious scheme.

Hidcote is the work of one man, Lawrence Johnston, an American, who created it from the bare Cotswold uplands over a period of forty years from 1907 onwards. Like Vita after him, he no

doubt consciously drew his inspiration from the manorial gardens of the past, with their lime walks, their alleys and avenues and bowers. It proved a very practical as well as visually compelling style for the exposed site. The tall hedges provide shelter within which plants grow unbuffeted by the wind, their fragrance captured in the still air of the garden 'rooms'. Within this garden framework, Major

shifting moods. The sharp tones of unfurling spring foliage and the bright little bulbs beneath the trees are thrown into relief by old stone walls or the warmer-seeming colours of mellow brick. As midsummer, hot perhaps but still with the lingering freshness of spring, passes into the sultry heat of high summer, the clean lines of wall and newly-trimmed hedge and path are a welcome antidote to the welter of colour, the abundant diversity of leaf and flower and the heavy greens of the tree canopy. The tints of autumn are never so vivid as when scarlet maple and golden birch leaves, red rowan berries and fiery barberry, flare against sombre clipped yew. And if winter's frosts prove too much for the fragile blooms of witch hazel and winter-

Johnston imposed a style of planting influenced both by the careless profusion of cottage gardens and the sophistication of the artist. Vita Sackville-West greatly admired Hidcote for this subtle blending of self-conscious artistry and cottage simplicity.

It is a style for all seasons, reassuringly solid and unchanging in its framework of hedges or walls, lawns, paths and paving, yet refreshingly alive in its

sweet and Christmas rose, still the garden is undefeated, its structure revealed in all its stark beauty.

Above all, this style is one which adapts itself with ease to gardens of much smaller compass, and this to a large degree explains why both Hidcote and Sissinghurst have been so extraordinarily influential and important in the history of twentieth-century garden design.

FORMAL PATTERN AND SHAPE

T HE URGE FOR ORDER CAN FIND EXPRESSION EVEN IN A SMALL SPACE. THERE NEED BE NO BRIGHT FLOWERS TO DISTRACT THE EYE; WHERE PATTERN AND FORM DOMINATE, THEY ARE BROUGHT TO LIFE BY THE PLAY OF LIGHT AND SHADOW AND THE SUBTLE VARIATIONS IN TEXTURE OF THE DIFFERENT PLANT COMPONENTS. IN THIS MODERN FORMAL GARDEN, DESIGNED BY SIR ROY STRONG, WITH A NICE TOUCH OF IRONY, THE STONE SCULPTURES AT THE CENTRE OF EACH 'KNOT' ALONE SPEAK OF THE FECUNDITY OF A GARDEN, THE URNS SPILLING OVER WITH CARVED GRAPES AND GOURDS.

LEFT: A garden that survives from the period of William of Orange is Levens Hall, Cumbria, made between 1690 and 1720. The topiary, made of green and golden yew and of box, has grown inexorably to massive dimensions, so that the pieces seem almost to jostle each other, set though they are each in their compartments surrounded by low, clipped edging.

ABOVE: We know that there were 'marvellous fair walks, [and] *topiarii operis'* at Haseley Court, Oxfordshire, in 1542. But the present topiary work, though the trees that form it were planted in 1850, was not clipped into shape until about 1900. The garden was neglected during the Second World War, but the topiary itself was kept immaculately clipped by an old gentleman from neighbouring Great Haseley, who called the pieces his 'kings and queens'.

The desire for formality has deep roots in the human psyche, stemming from the need to impose order on a hostile and threatening environment; the ability to appreciate untamed nature is a comparatively recent phenomenon, a luxury for those who feel secure. More recently still, nature untrammelled may become an escape from another kind of threat, that of the decaying urban environment. Perhaps this very modern sense of unease and insecurity accounts also for the resurgence in popularity of formal garden design. Once again, Paradise – or at least, its

earthly representation in gardens – is conceived of as a place of refuge, orderly and tranquil.

We know from archaeological evidence, and from the writings of the Roman Consul Pliny the Younger, who described his own Tuscan garden in considerable detail in the first century AD, that the pleasure gardens of Roman villas were laid out in formal designs, with clipped trees and shrubs, a fairly new fashion in his time. Between boxwood hedges, wrote Pliny, were 'box trees cut into all kinds of different shapes'. After the fall of the Roman Empire, several centuries passed during

LEFT: The great terraces of Powis are dwarfed by the Castle itself, to which they are linked by massive, clipped yews, each slightly different in outline, yet echoing, in their more or less rounded summits and vertical thrust, the shadowed arches of the middle terrace.

RIGHT: The setting of Powis Castle, in the Welsh hills, is spectacular, and its great hanging terraces have a monumentality and yet intimacy which are in perfect harmony with the surrounding country. A balustraded walk and belvedere are not only part of the design, but make the ideal point from which to view the misty autumn hills. The garden of Powis Castle dates from the early eighteenth century, and is one of the few in Britain to survive almost unchanged in design to this day. Though not in England, it looks to English gardens for its inspiration.

which gardening in Europe was regarded above all as a practical necessity. In other regions of the world – in China and Japan, in the vast territories reaching from Spain in the West to Samarkand and beyond in Central Asia and Bengal in South Asia in the east which were under Islamic rule – the garden continued to be an expression of the artistic impulse rooted in the spirituality of the dominant faith and the age. But in Europe, people cultivated the land to grow the food that fed peasant families, and nectar-rich flowers for the bees so they would be generous with their honey; the aromatic plants for strewing on the floor to keep foul odours at bay or to lay among linen and clothing to combat insect pests; the herbs that dyers used to tint their cloth or that skilled herbalists in monasteries needed to make ointments and physick to cure ills or alleviate pain. By the fifteenth century, living conditions – at least for the privileged – had greatly improved, and there came the first development of the Italian Renaissance, and soon thereafter the French, Dutch

and English garden styles: the garden as fine art rather than as utility.

In the sixteenth century, as for example in the England of the Tudors, topiary, knot gardens of elaborate design, and pleached trees were already popular. The style seemed, indeed, a natural development of the small *hortus inclusus*, which even in earlier days would have formed part of the mainly utilitarian gardens of the well-to-do, a place to sit in seclusion, with raised flower beds, turfed banks and seats aromatic with camomile and pennyroyal and thyme, all enclosed by wooden palings, hedges or walls of brick, stone or cob.

Formality remained the hallmark of gardens in the seventeenth century, with walled enclosures, arches and trellis and arbours, parterres, and fishponds. One of the finest examples of parterres and water was laid out at the palace of Hampton Court. In Holland the grandiose French formal garden style of Versailles or Vaux-le-Vicomte was tempered by the Dutch genius for domesticity, and when

RIGHT: Plant lovers know that Powis is renowned for the variety of its tender plants and the skill with which they are combined; but Powis also has its restrained moods, where the slight irregularities of outline in the clipped, living green wall of box that rises to the left are given full value for being allowed to speak for themselves without the busy intrusion of colour.

the Dutchman William of Orange gained the English throne in 1688 this Dutch garden style came with him. It suited the English temperament better than the magnificence of French gardens, influential though these had been on the wealthiest members of the nobility and gentry.

Gardens of this period in both Holland and England are characterized by patterns of canals, clipped trees and hedges, orangeries and pavilions, statuary, and more or less elaborate topiary. The most famous nurserymen of the early eighteenth century, when topiary was at its most popular, were the partners George London and Henry Wise, who used topiary extensively, much of it imported from Holland. Though box, once dominant for topiary, was still popular, the range of trees and shrubs used for topiary work increased; London and Wise also favoured bay, pyracantha, cherry laurel and *Phillyrea* (usually thought of as a Victorian favourite), and John Evelyn's *Sylva*, published in 1662, helped to popularize the use of yew. However, many topiary

ABOVE: Several of the great set-piece formal gardens of the seventeenth century have been preserved for posterity, not on the ground, but in the form of 'perspectives', painstakingly accurate bird's-eye illustrations of great houses and their gardens, such as Kip's or Kniff's engravings. Dating from 1699, Kniff's perspective of Chatsworth, Derbyshire, seat of the Dukes of Devonshire, shows that the garden of the first Duke, who owed his dukedom to his support for William of Orange, was parterred and statued in the high formal style. The fourth Duke succumbed to the eighteenth-century passion for idealized landscapes of the kind that belong in Chapter 3, but the Sea Horse and Triton fountains, the famous cascade, and the terracing survived. The bridge, spanning the river Derwent, dates from 1762. The sixth Duke restored some of Chatsworth's vanished formality in the nineteenth century, assisted by his garden superintendent Joseph Paxton, who was to become famous as the designer of London's Crystal Palace.

RIGHT: The Italian Renaissance garden was first conceived as a reconstruction of a classic grove. Perhaps there is a hint of this conscious reminder of a classic golden age in this statue, a herm, half-hidden by an embracing hedge at Chatsworth. For the men and women of the Renaissance, however, every statue of a mythical personage had a particular significance and symbolized a certain set of attributes. Today, most of us are left with only the purely aesthetic impact; we are deprived of the wealth of associations that were the common currency of a classical education.

ABOVE: The twentieth century has seen further development in the formal idiom at Chatsworth, including the four designs on the main terrace, of which this is one, composed of golden yew domes, candle-flames of Irish yew, obelisks of black-green yew, and geometric patterns of clipped box on curving stone plinths.

gardens of this period or earlier are restorations, not originals: Haseley and Chenies among them, using either trees and shrubs planted in the garden at a later date and then topiarized, or existing topiary work brought in from elsewhere (see pages 23 and 28). Very little original topiary survived the eighteenth century's idealized landscapes in which the formal had no place; and it may be, indeed, that the fashion for topiary was carried to excess. The poet

and gardener Alexander Pope, who was to be at the forefront of the change from the formal to the landscape style, wrote satirically, in 1713, of the kind of nonsense that topiarists loved to create: 'St George in box; his arm scarce long enough', and 'a green dragon of the same with a tail of ground-ivy', together with the delicious 'old Maid of Honour in wormwood'. And the essayist Joseph Addison wrote, in 1712, that 'British gardeners ... instead of

BELOW: At Chenies Manor, Buckinghamshire, the dark, clipped yew and box topiary, in which severity and cosiness seem to meet in equal proportions, set off a relaxed, all-white planting of dahlias, shasta daisies (*Leucanthemum × superbum*, better known as *Chrysanthemum maximum*) and phlox, with the pewter and silver foliage of artemisias. Chenies dates from Tudor times, but this topiary is relatively new to the garden, for it was rescued after the Second World War from a derelict nursery and replanted here. One of the four yew hens on her box nest was accidentally set facing the wrong way, her back to the statue of Cupid at the centre of the garden.

RIGHT: Haseley Court topiary in different mood from the 'kings and queens' seen on page 23, with a simple green and gold design as the setting for an aromatic, textured planting of green, glaucous-blue, grey and silver foliage – the leathery paddles of bergenia, the platinum velvet of lamb's ears (*Stachys byzantina*), blue rue, silvery santolina and Vatican sage (*Salvia sclarea* var. *turkestanica*), with its tall spires of mauve flowers. Several of the plants are aromatic, some of them pungently so – the Vatican sage has even earned itself the unkind and politically incorrect nickname 'hot housemaid', the reason quickly apparent to the refined nose when the plant is handled. The variations in colours and textures emphasize the design, and even the paths are patterned.

humouring nature, love to deviate from it as much as possible. We see the marks of scissors on every plant and bush'.

The highly formalized garden style, whether in the grand French manner of Le Nôtre's immense perspectives cut through the forests of the Ile de France, or in the more domesticated Dutch mode, lent itself less well to steep hillsides than to flat terrain or gentle slopes. To achieve it, a markedly sloping site would need to be terraced, and low hills could even be completely levelled, as happened, for example, at Chatsworth in Derbyshire, to make the south parterre and open up the fine view of the English countryside from the terraces (see page 27). The changes in level were also put to practical use to create the spectacular water features at Chatsworth, the famous Cascade and the fountains devised by the Frenchman Grillet (see also page 110).

ABOVE: Topiary is an art that goes back at least to Roman times in Britain, and has been in and out of fashion ever since. At Barnsley House, Gloucestershire, the simplest of topiary – a dome of golden privet (*Ligustrum ovalifolium* 'Aureum'), and a tiered holly – is set against a clean-cut beech hedge in its autumn livery.

LEFT: Orderly pairs of sentinel Irish yews, flanking this paved walk at Barnsley balance the exuberance of the pink, white and rose-red rock roses growing between the flagstones.

ABOVE: The miniature knot garden at Barnsley, made of two kinds of box, green and golden, with clipped germander, is composed of intricate patterns inspired by the formal designs of the past. In a frosted monochrome landscape, the imagination can take wing. This might indeed be a garden in Tudor England, framed in the landscape of fields, hedgerows and trees that centuries of careful husbandry have stamped upon the original wildness.

On very steep sites, a formal design with retaining walls, terraces and steps makes for a dramatic, rather than necessarily a grand garden. From the upper terrace there is likely to be an extensive view out over the surrounding country, as there is at Powis Castle (see pages 24–5), and at the same time the gaze is drawn downwards to the terraces and plantings below. The strong horizontal lines of terracing help to anchor the house and garden to the site, and to dispel the sense of instability, of falling, which a steep site can evoke.

Surviving gardens, archeological evidence, and books on horticulture and gardening may all help us to imagine or recreate the garden styles of the past. Reflecting the interest of Rosemary Verey, owner of Barnsley House, in garden history, the garden that surrounds the seventeenth-century manor house of honey-coloured Cotswold stone, is a compendium of garden styles, a living history book to echo Mrs Verey's extensive collection of old books on horticulture and garden design. It encompasses an Elizabethan knot garden, a *potager* in the formal French style, a quintessentially twentieth-century flower border, an eighteenth-century temple and a romantic wilderness of trees in meadow grass, a patterned herb garden and a lily-rimmed

LEFT: The Garden House, Buckland Monachorum, Devon, is set on a sloping site and is densely planted with a range of shrubs and trees that thrive on the acid soil and in the moist climate of this site at the edge of Dartmoor. What might otherwise be a rather formless collection of plants is given cohesion and structure by elements of formality within the design, as in this aperçu in a hedge of escallonia, where immaculately trimmed yew and cypress sentinels are set off by the white lace mantle of a spreading viburnum and the casual abundance of a wisteria.

pool. What holds this diversity of features together is an overarching simplicity of design in which the very English profusion of planting is held together by strong outlines. Clipped hedges, stone paving and cobbles, vistas leading to firm but quiet conclusions, expanses of lawn – these are the elements which form the palette of formality, handled with an unerring visual sense.

As we have seen, this blend of strong design and casual planting characterizes the best of twentieth-century English gardens. The formality of paving and clipped hedges and repetitive motifs both frames and lends coherence to the colourful, many-textured plantings which the English do so well, thanks to a benign climate which allows such a diversity of plants to thrive. Formal vistas draw the eye; but take a walk along the paved path or smooth lawn, and you will find yourself tempted by secret enclosures, planted with romantic profusion. These

secluded garden rooms not only provide shelter from the wind and a sense of privacy; they also serve in some measure to banish the outside world, their hedges muting the pervasive roar of the late twentieth century with its traffic-clogged roads and relentless industrial clatter. No more do we need to exclude hostile, encroaching nature; it is our own encroachments we seek refuge from today.

If the great set-piece gardens of Louis XIV's France, or even the less grandiose Dutch and English styles of the seventeenth century, were for the nobility, a more modest kind of formality was espoused from the end of the eighteenth century under the influence of the Picturesque movement, which was itself a kind of escapism, a harking back to an imaginary past when all was well with the world. It was, at the same time, a rejection both of the elaborately geometric French and Dutch style and of what F R Cowell has called 'the studied,

RIGHT: Formality using the simplest of elements – clipped hedges and box-edged squares, a fountain, lavender and roses – lends a sense of grandeur and timelessness to this private garden. The restraint suits the unpretentious house and allows the materials of which it is built to speak for themselves.

RIGHT: Frost picks out the patterns of this sunken formal garden designed by Rosemary Verey in Worcestershire, its box curlicues and interlacing knots contrasting with York paving. The golden stone of the house glows with warmth in an otherwise monochrome scene silvered by winter.

ABOVE: Topiary lends itself splendidly to levity and even irreverence. In this London garden designed by Dan Pearson, amid the chimney pots, an alert green bird – a duck, perhaps, though with the carriage of a swan – is perched on a nest of entwined branches, netting and bright baubles.

RIGHT: Topiary expresses and reflects its owner's passions, or topical events, as much as the vagaries of fashion. I recall, as a child in 1952, seeing a small front garden entirely filled by a throne – a rather formless one, it is true – clipped from the fast-growing *Lonicera nitida*, in honour of the coronation of Queen Elizabeth II. Squatting on a low hedge, these stylized bird forms in an Oxfordshire garden bear their shawls of snow calmly, lit by the low winter sun.

RIGHT: In this garden in
Avon a gondola and a steam
locomotive have been
lovingly carved and
immaculately maintained
in privet.

mannered indifference of plain English landscape effects'. The Picturesque began as an aesthetic movement, most famously expressed in Sir Uvedale Price's *Essay on the Picturesque* of 1794; but it was to become a typically nineteenth-century trend in Britain; the gentry would play at the rustic life, building cottage-like dwellings – though with none of the inconveniences of true cottage life – with gardens where they sought to evoke an idyllic, imaginary past. Cottages for the gentry were built in self-consciously vernacular style, with thatched roofs and wide, overhanging eaves, or in the Old English style in stone or half-timbered brick. These gothic-inspired dwellings, in particular, would be surrounded by gardens that sought to echo in more simple manner the formal Tudor style. Although it did not give rise to a new garden style as such, at its best the Picturesque was a major strand in the development of one of the most enduring English garden styles of the second half of the twentieth century, the romanticized, sophisticated cottage garden – of which we shall see more in Chapter 9.

It was to a large extent true cottagers, unmoved by the whims of fashion which dictated that formal gardens be swept away to be replaced by contoured landscapes, who kept up the art of topiary in Britain. Robert Southey, friend of the romantic poets Wordsworth and Coleridge, described a yeoman's garden in Yorkshire which 'you entered between two yew trees clipt to the fashion of two pawns', and he confessed that 'Even the clipt yews interest me; and if I found one in any garden that should be mine, in the shape of a peacock, I should be as proud to keep his tail well spread as the man who first carved him'. This humble topiary was reclaimed by the Picturesque movement and, later in the nineteenth century, by the Arts and Crafts Movement; while highly formal geometric topiary often featured in Edwardian gardens. Box and yew remain the shrubs of choice for topiary work, lending themselves to the grand style of Levens Hall (see page 22), to the traditional shapes of ball, pyramid and spiral (see page 134), to stylized peacocks on plinths, to the artless cockyolly birds or castellated hedges of cottage gardens, and to the present-day confections of the enthusiast or the cheerfully self-mocking.

THE TAMED
LANDSCAPE

The eighteenth century, the age of reason, is exemplified in English gardens by coolly rational, even emotionless landscapes of grass and trees and water, decorated by temples and bridges of purest classical style. At the Royal Botanic Gardens, Kew, on the outskirts of London, the Temple of Bellona, built by the architect Sir William Chambers in the 1760s, in early spring looks down not on cropped grass as was originally intended, but on an expanse of purple and white crocuses that were planted in the 1980s.

ABOVE: The garden at Stourhead, Wiltshire, is at its most beautiful in the early morning or evening light. Its creator, the banker Henry Hoare, must have been a man of rare vision to imagine the empty valley filled with water and the bare Wiltshire downs clad with trees, and therein to place temples, grottoes and bridges with so sure an eye. Beginning in 1740, he dammed two valleys to create a great lake, spanned at its narrow point by this simple, beautifully proportioned bridge, of which Henry Hoare wrote, 'I took it from Palladio's bridge at Vicenza'. The rhododendrons are a nineteenth-century introduction.

However eager English gardeners may be to acquire new plants, they have tended, throughout the later twentieth century, to be resolutely traditional in matters of garden design. But with such a variety of traditions to look back upon, there is a great diversity of garden styles in England today. There are the great surviving landscape gardens of the eighteenth century, to be sure, and traces, or recent restorations, of the formal set-pieces that the landscape gardens supplanted. Of the twentieth century itself there are the Lutyens gardens of which so many smaller, newer gardens are a wistful echo; there are woodland gardens, where plants that Nature absent-mindedly evolved in different continents now grow side by side in a leafy and eclectic Eden; and there are the self-conscious cottage gardens, modest descendants perhaps of Hidcote and Sissinghurst. Typically, late twentieth-century gardens in England are derivative; and with so rich a heritage to draw upon, they could hardly be otherwise. If there is a new style, it

is perhaps the 'ecological' – the garden where plants are asssociated according to their needs rather than on purely aesthetic grounds. Meadow gardening, where flowers are naturalized in grass, belongs here; some meadows gardeners are purists, growing only wild flowers, while others add exotics, plants from subalpine or Himalayan slopes or American prairies.

From the time gardens first became more than merely utilitarian, they have been conceived as idealized landscapes, as a refuge from nature, and

RIGHT: The coppery foliage of beeches frames Stourhead's Temple of the Sun, mirrored in the still waters of the lake. The temple is said to be modelled on one at Baalbec. The genius of Henry Hoare is all the more remarkable in that he created Stourhead before the advent of the landscape school of gardener-poet William Shenstone and Capability Brown; indeed, he began it even before the landscapes on canvas of Claude and Poussin became popular in Britain, in the mid eighteenth century.

LEFT: The *raison d'être* of the Palladian Bridge spanning this small piece of water at Stowe, Buckinghamshire, is far more aesthetic than functional. The grounds of Stowe, seat of Sir Richard Temple, Viscount Cobham, were the most famous of their kind in eighteenth-century England. They were originally planned by Charles Bridgeman and taken over by William Kent, who – in Horace Walpole's famous phrase – 'leaped the fence and saw that all Nature was a garden'. From him Capability Brown learned much; for it was at Stowe that Brown worked after completing his seven years' apprenticeship as a gardener's boy.

ABOVE: The grounds at Stowe were inspired by the Roman school of Italian and French paysagistes. But the influence of the poet Alexander Pope, who greatly admired Stowe, was also strong; his notion of the 'genius of the place' was respected, and Stowe remained essentially English. This Temple of British Worthies contains busts of such famous Englishmen as Shakespeare.

RIGHT: This statue of Hercules at Hidcote seems to be gazing down at the sheep that lie, in pastoral confidence, at its feet. Hidcote is, of course, primarily a garden of enclosed spaces from which the landscape has been excluded by high hedges. It it is the sky, rather than the surrounding country, to which the eye is led. But Hidcote has its reminiscences of other styles; the classical, as in this quiet corner, and even its own woodland-in-Eden.

RIGHT BELOW: The hard, clean lines of a stone balustrade and pillar in the garden at Saling Hall, Essex are softened by piles of fallen autumn leaves. The contrast between the durability and solidity of stone and the transience, the imminence of decay of the foliage heightens the sense of nostalgia which accompanies even the most golden of autumn days.

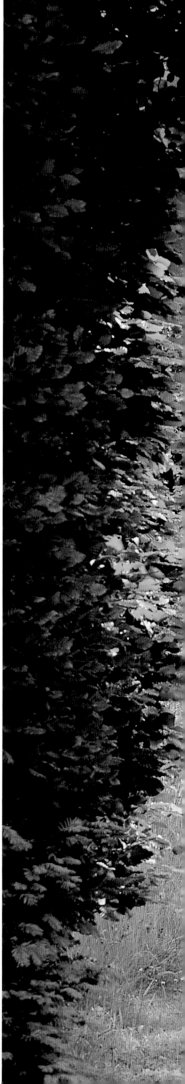

later as its perfect expression. It was agriculture that first tamed the landscape; but as the European landscape became increasingly subjugated to human needs, the wildness of remote heath and moorland, of mountains and streams and ancient forests, came to have a strong emotive appeal to people endowed with leisure, the means to travel and a degree of sensibility. Gardens, too, began to change; in place of the ordered formality of the Dutch style or the opulent grandeur of the French, it was the classic ideal landscape of painters such as Poussin and Claude Lorrain which became the inspiration for English gardens. Alexander Pope (1688–1744), as remarkable a gardener as he was a poet, was a key figure in the 'improving' movement.

The eighteenth-century professional landscape designers William Kent (1884–1748) and Lancelot 'Capability' Brown (1715–1783) imagined the ideal in serene classical simplicity, with contoured parkland, carefully disposed clumps and belts of native trees, and lakes. The old, flowery gardens had no place in this vision; instead, close-mown lawns, free of the distraction of flower beds or clipped hedges, ran right to the very walls of the stately houses they adorned, and the device of the ha-ha (a ditch and retaining wall or sunken fence) between the lawn and the surrounding parkland or fields gave the illusion that the lawn merged imperceptibly into the distant, controlled landscape. Temples, bridges spanning the streams that fed the lakes, and statuary, completed the classical illusion. One of the finest surviving examples of a classical landscape of this kind is at Stowe, in Buckinghamshire.

Now that they are mature, these designed landscapes seem not only natural, but timeless. It was an extraordinary feat of the imagination to plant saplings of elm or oak or chestnut and visualize how they would look two centuries later; in his day Brown's landscapes must have seemed spartan in the extreme. And indeed, very soon after his death there was a reaction against them, against the way in which grand old avenues and formal terraces alike had been swept away.

There were changing fashions in plants as well as in landscape design at this time. During the eighteenth and, above all, the nineteenth centuries, more and more exotic plants were introduced into European gardens. The aromatics of southern Europe, the bulbs of the Central Asian silk route and the prairie flowers of North America were joined by many new flowering trees and shrubs in the nineteenth century. Native trees were joined by exotics: Japanese cherries and maples, Himalayan and Chinese magnolias and rowans, American oaks, and much else besides. The modest selection of native British evergreen shrubs – holly, box and

LEFT: One of the simplest ways of taming a piece of the landscape is to close-mow a path through a flowery meadow sward, as here at Penns in the Rocks, Sussex, where the arch cut through a beech hedge is echoed in the natural vault of trees at the woodland's edge, framing a classic urn at the end of the vista.

LEFT: The English have drawn freely upon other traditions to decorate their gardens. Some elements they absorb, others remain recognizably foreign; among them, the garden architecture which copies, or is inspired by, the classical tradition, as are so many fine English buildings. This little temple, with its plain Doric-style columns and unadorned pediment, stands between busts of Queen Victoria and Prince Albert at the end of a long vista in a private garden designed by Sir Roy Strong; it seems perfectly at ease with its very English setting of roses on blue-painted trellis.

ABOVE: With the simplest of materials, the garden at Bramdean House, Hampshire, evokes an idealized English spring landscape. Housman's woodland cherry or gean, 'hung with bloom along the bough ... wearing white for Eastertide', has metamorphosed into these billowing mounds of snowy blossom, their flounces contrasting strongly with their dark, slender Irish yew companions; and Wordsworth's 'host of golden daffodils', the frail-seeming Lent lily of west-country English hedgerows, *Narcissus pseudonarcissus*, has been replaced by a brighter, more assertive horde of wide-cupped narcissi in white and yellow and orange, naturalized in grass.

OVERLEAF: The fritillary meadows of Magdalen College, Oxford, are renowned. For the graceful snakeshead fritillary to grow in such profusion, the meadows must have been managed, probably for centuries, with the utmost simplicity: no fertilizers or herbicides, and merely a cut after midsummer, once the seeds have ripened and fallen, with another perhaps in early autumn. *Fritillaria meleagris*, its hanging, chequered bells varying from shades of murrey to alabaster-white, is a plant of moist meadows, but in these days of chemically-induced lushness and uniformity in the meadows where cattle graze, it is more often seen in gardens than in the fields.

yew – was extended with Mexican orange, Californian lilac, spotted laurel, and above all rhododendrons in dazzling variety. These alone were to produce an almost cult-like following which endures to this day, some aficionados seeking brighter, hardier hybrids tough enough to grow anywhere, others preferring the more subtle charms of the species growing in sheltered woodland. Even the gardens of Stourhead – a classical landscape *par excellence*, with lakes, temples, and sculpted woodlands – saw their contoured banks of laurel felled to be replaced and extended by rhododendrons. For one month in every twelve, the integrity of the original landscape is violated by the intrusion of brilliant colour which had no place in the original concept of its creator.

The classical landscape, then, was unsuited to growing these newly-introduced plants, many of which were strikingly beautiful or irresistibly tempting to the collector of curiosities. The old favourite flowers, too, banished to the kitchen garden or cottager's plot, were coming back into favour: cottage paeonies and oriental poppies, bellflowers and gilliflowers and columbines. A new garden style, a new vision of the idealized landscape was needed, to enable countless gardeners, whether in expansive acres, in town villas or in cottage plots, to plant their personal Edens.

Neither the formality of the French or Dutch styles nor the plain English landscape could meet the new mood of sensuous enjoyment that was manifesting itself in art, in literature – and in gardening. The exotically romantic garden came into being, with Humphrey Repton as its greatest English exponent. Repton, a landowning gentleman who lost his independent means and was obliged to earn his living, was initially an admirer of Brown, but under the influence of Sir Uvedale Price, author of *Essay on the Picturesque*, he came to see a garden 'not as a landscape but as a work of art using the materials of nature'. He demonstrated his ideas to prospective clients in his 'red books' where, using colour sketches and overlays, he created before-and-after impressions of each site.

Repton advocated an 'artificial garden, richly clothed with flowers and decorated with statues and works of art', which should be visible from the

ABOVE: The flower-spangled meadows, still evident in the 1950s, bright with buttercups and daisies, cowslips and lady's smock, are rarities today, casualties of modern farming methods. But a growing number of gardeners are recreating the flowery mead, as here at Hadspen Garden, Somerset, where a close-mown path is formed at the meadow's edge to curve tantalizingly away out of sight, and where tulips have been planted to join the buttercups and daisies in the grass.

house as the 'rich frame of the landscape'. He did not hesitate to make use of such contrivances as the ha-ha whenever, beyond the lawn and the confines of the garden proper, there lay a landscape that could be 'borrowed', if need be by removing a tree or copse that obscured the view. If there was no suitable view, the garden could be made to seem larger by laying paths which curved away out of sight; while if at worst there was an eyesore to conceal, a carefully placed tree, or a garden house, could be brought into service. Though its expression was different from that of Kent and Brown, the impulse was the same: to create an idealized landscape, a vision of Eden on earth. In place of the simplicity of

RIGHT ABOVE: Gardeners can be terribly earnest at times; but why should not humour be part of our stamp on the landscape? In the half-wild garden at Heligan, Cornwall, a fallen log is transmogrified into a beast leaping, mouth agape, from the undergrowth.

RIGHT BELOW: Woven from living willow, another leaping beast bears a fine head of green and leafy antlers. Perhaps there is something in the West Country air that provokes these whimsies – this creature is to be found in Stone Lane Gardens, Devon.

LEFT: The mild climate and high humidity of the south-west of England are ideal for lush, jungly plantings such as this, at The Lost Garden of Heligan, Cornwall, with gunnera and the great fronds of tree ferns, lit by the dappled sunlight that filters through the tree canopy. These gardens, overgrown after long neglect, are being reclaimed and restored.

the classical landscape, however, Repton stressed variety; henceforth there would no longer be one dominant style, and the diversity of design was soon to be echoed in the wide variety of plants grown in England's gardens.

Britain's gardeners are, of course, almost uniquely fortunate in their climate. Without the benign influence of the Gulf Stream, which warms the island shores and produces the endlessly variable weather that, in sum, amounts to an equable climate suitable for a wide variety of plants, the gardens of these isles would have been, no doubt, more uniform and less idiosyncratic. As it is, out of the eclectic borrowing from the world's flora more than

one distinctively British style of gardening has emerged. The western shores offer a congenial home for plants from the lusher, wetter regions of the world, provided only that shelter be contrived against the buffeting, salt-laden westerly winds. In the south-east, Kent has an almost continental climate, with plenty of sun in summer and sharper, more defined, though still relatively mild, winters. This seasonal pattern suits fruit trees, hops and vines well: no wonder the county as a whole is known as the Garden of England. And the great cities – London above all – are urban heat islands which allow for a wide range of Mediterranean and even subtropical plants to thrive unprotected.

ABOVE: Step back from the balustrade at Saling Hall, (illustrated on page 42), and you see a woodland scene with a small pool, mysterious as only shadowed, leaf-strewn water can be. Around the pool, the foliage of hostas, irises and ferns, lush all summer in the glancing shadows of the trees, echoes the golden maple leaves as they turn to buff and russet with the onset of autumn and the first crisp nights.

The moist, mild climate of the western coastal regions, from Cornwall northwards along the Welsh coast to the Western Isles of Scotland, is the *raison d'être* of a particular style of planting, lush and dense, with a jungle quality of foliage beneath a canopy of trees that absorbs and deflects the fierce Atlantic gales, as at The Lost Garden of Heligan in Cornwall (see opposite). On a windy day, in these gardens, the hush as one passes from an open place to the shelter of the trees is palpable; overhead the branches are whipped by the force of the wind, but beneath all is still and calm. At times in summer the wind drops, there is not a breath of air, and the sun beats down with almost tropical intensity; the open garden is bleached with heat, but in the embrace of the trees there is coolness and shade. Here the wide blades of hostas, the great paddles of bog arum, the lacy fronds of ferns, the massively pleated, rough-textured leaves of gunnera remain fresh and green until winter claims them.

In the drier east of the country, salt-laden gales are less the problem than icy or searingly dry winds from the east, whipping across from the huge land-mass of northern Eurasia. The answer, once again, is shelter, in the shape of tree plantings which may evoke the great oak or beech forests that once covered so much of the British Isles. Tamed and domesticated, these primeval forests-in-little are

LEFT: Kiftsgate Court, Gloucestershire, is very close to Hidcote Manor, and the garden was begun at much the same time. As at Hidcote, the different parts of the garden are frequently based on a definite colour theme; but the overall design is less strictly formal. Here, orange and yellow Welsh poppies (*Meconopsis cambrica*) have seeded themselves between shrubs and trees.

BELOW: This simple picture evokes the landscape-as-Eden. A close-mown path cuts a swathe through a scattering of daffodils in the grass, all lit by spring sunlight, in a private garden.

LEFT: The woodland-as-Eden is an enduring theme in British gardens. Lovely though a native woodland may be, the temptation to add to its restricted palette is strong; and in an idealized woodland, nature can be given a helping hand to achieve subtle or striking associations of flower and foliage. Here at Vann, Surrey, shuttlecock ferns (*Matteuccia struthiopteris*) and the bronzed, boldly web-footed *Rodgersia podophylla* grow with the yellow honeysuckle azalea, (*Rhododendron luteum*), and the snowball tree, (*Viburnum ppulus* 'Roseum'). Despite the presence of exotics from several different regions, the restrained use of colour ensures harmony with the natural woodland scene.

another variant on the Eden landscape, at their most enchanting in spring when the little flowers of the understorey – native wood anemones, prim-roses, sweet violets, and exotic woodlanders from North America or China or Japan, like Virginian cowslip and wake robin, trout lily and bloodroot and dawn poppy – burst into bloom for that brief moment when the warmth of the sun spurs every-thing into growth and before the leaves of the trees exclude much of its light. Another moment of glory comes in autumn when the dying foliage of the trees flares into bonfire colours as at Saling Hall in Essex (see page 51). The scarlet of maples and American oaks, the russet of the native British oak, the flame and crimson and purple of rowans, the gold of birches and the smoky pink of the katsura, with its fallen leaves wafting a smell of hot toffee. The soft-er climate of the western coasts does not produce such autumn pyrotechnics.

It needs vigilance to maintain the balance of light and shade, of shelter and air, for a woodland garden to remain at its best, as it is at Vann, in Surrey (see

opposite); for trees grow, mature and die, like any liv-ing thing, and as they grow the shade beneath them deepens, from the dappled shadow and glancing light of young trees to the deep, mossed shade of a mature forest. It may be necessary to let in more light, by selective branch reduction, or even the removal of entire trees; to create glades and paths so you can admire at close quarters the butterfly blooms of the honeysuckle azalea and submit to the swooning perfume they exhale. These delights, of course, cannot thrive except on lime-free soil, leafy and moist. The paradise woodland on chalk soil calls for different treatment. Here whitebeams will thrive, unfurling their grey velvet leaves like chalices in spring, and cherries in pure white, blush, or even, in sugar pink. Beneath their canopy you may enjoy the lacy, white mantles of the guelder rose (*Viburnum opulus*) with wood sorrel, dog's tooth violet, Welsh poppies and darkly-fingered *Helleborus foetidus*, lily-of-the-valley and bluebells. There is much to console the gardener who would make a woodland-in-Eden on chalky soil.

THE CLASSIC FLOWER BORDER

IN THE FLOWER BORDER AS CAPTIVE RAINBOW, THE MOST DIFFICULT TRANSITION IS THAT FROM PINKS AND MAUVES TO THE STRONG YELLOWS AND THE HOT ORANGES, SCARLET AND CRIMSON. HERE, AT THE PRIORY, KEMERTON, HEREFORD AND WORCESTER, THE GRADING OF COLOUR HAS BEEN ACCOMPLISHED WITH RARE SKILL. IT IS HELPED BY THE COOL, JADE-GREEN DUVETS OF SEDUMS, THE BASS NOTES OF PURPLE FOLIAGE AND THE USE OF CONTRASTING FOLIAGE LINES TO CAPTURE THE GAZE OR TO IMPEL IT ONWARDS. THE VIVID MASS AT THE CENTRE IS COMPOSED OF RED HOT POKERS, SCARLET DAHLIAS AND CRIMSON BERGAMOT AND TOBACCO FLOWERS, FIERY ORANGE CROCOSMIAS AND YELLOW DAISIES, WITH THE PUCKERED LEAVES OF RUBY CHARD.

The great contribution of the early twentieth century to English gardens is the herbaceous border. Borders of hardy flowers were not unknown before the Edwardian era; but it was now that perennials came into their own again as components of a new design element. In the immaculately-tended walled kitchen gardens of great houses and the little plots of cottagers alike, hardy flowering plants had survived the eighteenth-century fashion for flowerless landscapes and the Victorian passion for parterres of exotic bedding plants, to be reclaimed when their time came again. What we have now come to think of as the traditional herbaceous border, containing the classic border perennials – delphiniums, shasta daisies, oriental poppies, gaillardias, heleniums, phlox and the like, with asters and chrysanthemums to end the season's display – was a summer spectacular with nothing to show for itself at other seasons. It was also very labour-intensive; in the best-regulated gardens, the entire border would be annually double-trenched and manured, the plants divided and the strong outer growths reset for the following year's display. Few people nowadays have the means or inclination to make such an effort for so brief a display, and borders today tend to be mixed rather than purely herbaceous. Once again, the inspiration is Miss Jekyll. When she designed her main flower border at Munstead, with its carefully graded colours, she was experimenting and innovating, not only in the use of colour as such but in the best ways to use the well-loved flowers of summer so as to create the beautiful pictures to which she always aspired. She believed that 'the purpose of a garden is to give happiness and repose of mind ..., and to give it through the representation of the best kind of pictorial beauty of flower and foliage that can be combined or invented. And I think few people will deny that this kind of happiness is much more often enjoyed in the contemplation of the homely border of hardy flowers than in many of these great gardens, where the flowers ... have to take a lower rank as mere masses of colour filling so many square yards of space'. (*Wall and Water Gardens.*)

It calls for both plantsmanship and aesthetic sensitivity of a high order to recreate a Jekyll border, and this is especially so where space is limited. Miss

Jekyll herself was blessed, of course, not only with great artistic gifts, but with the means to express them in her garden: the main border was two hundred feet long and fourteen feet wide, space enough to use generous drifts of each plant. The word 'drift' suggests a long, thin planting rather than a block of each plant; as Miss Jekyll wrote, 'it not only has a more pictorial effect, but a thin long planting does not leave an unsightly empty space when the flowers are done and the leaves have perhaps died down.' An older style of herbaceous border, is designed around blocks of one kind of plant rather than drifts. Though adjacent groups may be chosen for their harmonious or deliberately contrasting colours, there is no overall graduated scheme of the kind Miss Jekyll devised, and which can be seen for example, at Tintinhull House (see pages 70–1), or, splendidly, at The Priory,

Kemerton, the creation of the late Peter Healing, who achieved the crescendo of colour illustrated on pages 54–5 and the softer tones seen on page 65.

Although people still talk of the 'herbaceous border', Miss Jekyll's main border, then, was already closer to the modern notion of a mixed border, at least as regards its components; indeed she herself called it a 'mixed border of hardy flowers', which contained shrubs, bulbs, half-hardy annuals and bedding plants as well as flowering perennials. She designed it as a rainbow of colour, static and perfect in its short season. In this her idea of the border was aesthetically and, one might argue, philosophically closer to the French concept of a garden as a static artifact than to the ever-changing English garden with its fugitive pleasures as the seasons come and go and its trees, shrubs and hedges grow, mature and lapse into senescence. Even with a variety of plants, set in drifts, and supplemented with her 'contrivances' of teasing the stems of a late-flowering plant over the empty space left by an early-blooming one, or popping in potsful of hydrangeas, lilies and the like, she acknowledged that 'it is impossible to keep any one flower border fully dressed for the whole summer'. And that was with a large garden staff to deal with the regular lifting, dividing, resetting, manuring, staking and cutting-back that such a border demanded if it was to remain in good heart.

ABOVE: The double herbaceous borders at Arley Hall, Cheshire, are among the oldest in Britain. Among their most striking features are the stepped buttresses of clipped yew that divide the borders into sections, with topiary work atop the backing hedge echoing the stone finials to the left and more topiary standing sentinel at either end. These give a firm framework and rhythm to a flowery planting of cloudy outlines in which soft or unassertive colours dominate.

LEFT: The planting in the Arley Hall herbaceous borders is based on clumps, rather than drifts, of each plant; but care is given to associations of both colour and form. Here the deep blue of soaring delphinium spikes and the cumulus mounds of paler blue-lavender *Campanula lactiflora* are paired with lemon yellow anthemis and the tall spires of yellow foxtail lily (*Eremurus*), and the glaucous-blue globes of opium poppy seed heads. The block of stark white allows for touches of scarlet, from the poppies, and magenta-crimson to infiltrate the group without violence to the eye.

RIGHT: The cottage garden at Sissinghurst is planted with flowers of warm sunset tones, orange and apricot and tan, with the sharp acid yellows of spurges, flat plates of yellow achillea set off by their own feathery silver foliage, the broader silver leaves and white-felted flower spikes of mullein, yellow irises, great drifts of red and yellow columbines, and oxblood-scarlet roses. The centrepiece is a flower-filled old copper, green with the verdigris of age, filled with scarlet musk. As elsewhere at Sissinghurst, the generous informality of the planting is balanced by formal lines, and above all by the columnar Irish yews at the centre of the little garden.

ABOVE: Tulips and forget-me-nots wake up the borders at Tintinhull House, Somerset. In the predominantly green setting of emerging spring foliage, the scarlet and orange-vermilion of the tulips stand out vividly, while drifts of black-purple tulips are more discreet. Even a border which is designed to be at its peak in summer can look good earlier in the year, if bulbs are planted among the perennials which will flower later.

ABOVE: A garden door opens onto a border packed with the flowers of summer in this private garden. The gently harmonizing colours of delphiniums in azure, ultramarine and lavender are set off by pink roses and touches of lemon yellow, given sparkle by the white roses scaling the silvery-grey wall that backs the border. Pansies, *Heuchera* 'Palace Purple' and pink diascias form the petticoat frill at the front of the border.

RIGHT: In the warm light of early morning, the same border, looking the other way, just a little later in the year, with pink and maroon daylilies, blue globe thistles, pink mallow, *Campanula lactiflora* and white verbascums maintaining the gentle colour scheme. The buttresses of yew that punctuate the border add firmness of structure and a repetitive rhythm.

Furthermore, her garden was large enough to allow for different areas to be at their peak at different seasons, so she consciously planted this great border to be at its best in the late summer. Until then, from spring onwards the border was well filled with foliage, if not flower – the fresh foliage of late-flowering perennials, the haze of grey foliage at either end and the strong lines of yuccas – and lit by incidents: bearded irises, violet-purple *Geranium* x *magnificum* and oriental poppies in June. It is here that we see the principle advantage of the mixed over the purely herbaceous border.

Another great artist of the border, a contemporary of ours, Christopher Lloyd, uses colour very differently from Miss Jekyll, though with no less acute an aesthetic sensitivity. In his garden at Great Dixter, in Kent, blocks and drifts of colour come and go amid shrubs chosen for their substance, their foliage, their outline; the border gives the impression of having evolved year by year, as a group that he likes forms the germ of an idea and is expanded. As you walk along the paved path – over which the plants at the front of the border flop and flow in pleasant indiscipline – your eye is caught time and again by a plant association that you long to plagiarize (most dedicated garden visitors carry a notebook, in which shamelessly to crib successful plant combinations, themes, and ideas).

The conventional border is backed by a wall or a hedge. In Miss Jekyll's garden, the wall behind her border was clothed with 'shrubs and plants that take their place in the colour scheme, either for tint of bloom or mass of foliage'. They were there for their visual effect, not because they needed the shelter of the wall to survive or to bloom. The Long Border at Great Dixter is set in front of high yew hedges, a sombre dark green backdrop for the bright colours. Informal plantings, whether carefully colour-coordinated or casually haphazard, may be enhanced by the clean lines of a box-edged bed or border; or a border of flowers may be punctuated with buttresses or divisions of clipped yew or box, giving an air of stability and rhythm to the often cloudy insubstantiality of border flowers. Some of the most successful examples of this are to be seen in the gardens of Powis Castle (see pages 74 and 77), and the borders of Arley Hall (see page 57).

LEFT: At Court House, East Quantoxhead, Somerset, dominating the foreground is a three-colour group of scarlet penstemons, the soft yellow perennial foxglove *Digitalis grandiflora*, and the violet-purple spikes of flowering sage. The paved path yields to a grassy walk, which needs careful management to avoid these soft, billowy outlines being massacred by the mower and edge trimmer. There are, of course, neat and compact edging plants; but used alone, they risk looking insufferably prim, and are best associated with front-of-the-border plants that are low and spreading. Where the border runs alongside a hard-surfaced path – paving, rolled gravel, setts, or brick – the plants can be allowed to flop unhindered, naturally forming their own soft, flowing outlines. If the border adjoins a lawn or grass path, a band of mowing stones or of mellowed bricks, between the border edge and the grass, set just below the level of the grass, gives a finished appearance to the border as well as allowing the plants at the front to flop without being damaged by the mower.

ABOVE: In the same garden, a border raised a few inches above the level of the stone path is retained by a low stone wall, the ideal place for spreading plants to loll. The stone provides not only a defined edge to the border but also a visual emollient to the strong, quarrelling colours in this group: scarlet-flowered *Penstemon pinifolius*, the bright blue spikes of a veronica and the taller spires of purple-flowered sage, a yellow-variegated euonymus and the mauve-pink of daisy-flowered erigerons and penstemon.

Perennials and their accompanying cast of shrubs, bulbs and annuals need not be grown only in borders. The rival style of 'island beds' has been pioneered by Alan Bloom; he both wrote persuasively about perennials and their use and put his theories to practical test in the island beds at Bressingham in Norfolk. These are, in effect, double-sided borders of informal outline, with smaller plants at the margins and the taller ones at the centre or along the spine of the bed.

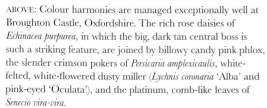

ABOVE: Colour harmonies are managed exceptionally well at Broughton Castle, Oxfordshire. The rich rose daisies of *Echinacea purpurea*, in which the big, dark tan central boss is such a striking feature, are joined by billowy candy pink phlox, the slender crimson pokers of *Persicaria amplexicaulis*, white-felted, white-flowered dusty miller (*Lychnis coronaria* 'Alba' and pink-eyed 'Oculata'), and the platinum, comb-like leaves of *Senecio vira-vira*.

LEFT: At Broughton Castle the stone that edges the lawn has aesthetic value as well as practical use, its pale, silvery colouring emphasizing the soft shades of pink and purple and blue, well leavened with white, that compose this section of border. Penstemons and potentillas provide the shades of pink and crimson, delphiniums the blues; the deep garnet-red pincushions in the foreground belong to the scabious-like *Knautia macedonica*.

ABOVE: The Priory, Kemerton, Hereford and Worcester, is renowned for its colour borders in which tender plants such as this shaggy pink dahlia, and annuals like the tall white cosmos behind it, are such an important feature. The butterfly plant in the foreground is a richly-coloured form of *Sedum spectabile*, its intense crimson-pink seeming to advance towards the eye. The pink tones of the dahlia and roses yield to blue-mauve Michaelmas daisies which, with their cool, recessive tones, emphasize the length of what is a comparatively small border.

RIGHT: The alternating round and square pillars of this old pergola at Little Thakeham, Sussex (a Lutyens house), disappear into a flower-packed planting on either side of a paved path. In the foreground, skin-pink and coral achilleas face the vivid magenta-flowered dusty miller, which is repeated further down the opposite border; clear yellow daylilies and the lime-green columns of *Euphorbia characias wulfenii* add an astringent note. By comparison with the profuse planting at ground level, the pergola itself is left almost unadorned; its wooden cross-beams, silvered with age, are handsome in their own right.

LEFT: Double, facing borders are also to be seen at Tintinhull House, Somerset. Paths of different textures – gravel leading in one direction, stone paving in the other – intersect between these twin borders in which pink roses and purple catmint predominate, enlivened by the branching spires of yellow mullein and by the slender, almost leafless stems topped by violet posies of *Verbena bonariensis*. Draped over the clipped yew arch, and just visible top left, are the burnt-orange, lopsided bugles of the Chilean glory flower (*Eccremocarpus scaber*), while the chartreuse-green froth of lady's mantle (*Alchemilla mollis*) softens the steps below. Beyond, a white rambling rose, with flowering grasses at its feet, frames a stone vase.

Chapter 5 is devoted to questions of colour, so here I invite you to regard primarily outline, form, and texture. Just as much as colours, these elements of design can complement or contrast with each other, harmonize or compete. Consider the cloudy outlines of starry-flowered *Aster sedifolius*, the duvet-like masses of *Sedum spectabile*, the fuzzy haze of *Thalictrum aquilegifolium* and the fluff of meadow-

LEFT: A planting of silver, pink and white by a sunny wall at Broughton Castle, Oxfordshire. Colours have a marked influence on our moods, and a few moments' pause on the sun-warmed wood of the bench will be doubly restful on account of the calming colours around it – to say nothing of the fragrance of the roses, and of the sweet rocket behind the bench.

RIGHT: By comparison with the formality implicit in double borders, this raised border at Ashtree Cottage, Wiltshire evokes a typically unselfconscious cottage scene, with blue and white peach-leaved bellflowers (*Campanula persicifolia*), pink roses, blue flax and meadow cranesbill, blue-leafed *Mertensia simplicissima* and a variety of little oddments including dark pink scabious tucked in at the front.

sweet, the foam of *Alchemilla mollis*, the pyramids of *Campanula lactiflora* or of peppery-scented phlox that, in the mass, make billowing mounds. Other plants are emphatically horizontal: notably achilleas, with their flat plate-like heads. All these contrast with strongly upward-thrusting outlines: the spires and steeples of delphiniums and monkshoods, acanthus, *Lythrum*, lupins; the pokers of pink bistort and kniphofias, the plumes of astilbes, the narrow wands of cimicifuga, the broad columns of *Euphorbia characias wulfenii*. Arching sprays belong to *Crocosmia masoniorum*, spiky ruffs to eryngiums. Then there are the globes of alliums, large and yet airy in *A. christophii*, smaller and denser in *A. giganteum* and its kind; the spherical heads of agapanthus or the smaller globe thistles; the full-packed roundness of cottage and double Chinese peonies and double

LEFT: Penelope Hobhouse, who created or developed several of the planting schemes at Tintinhull House, Somerset, has made a particular study of colour, as did Gertrude Jekyll before her. In *Colour Schemes for the Flower Garden*, Miss Jekyll devoted a chapter to gardens of special colouring, in which she wrote that 'a blue garden, for beauty's sake, may be hungering for a group of white Lilies, or for something of palest lemon-yellow ... it should be beautiful first, and then just as blue as may be consistent with its best possible beauty. Moreover, any experienced colourist knows that the blues will be more telling – more purely blue – by the juxtaposition of rightly placed complementary colour.' The amber-yellow bearded irises among the blue love-in-the-mist (*Nigella* 'Miss Jekyll') prove the point, and the touches of mauve from the alliums and magenta from the Byzantine gladiolus bring a further sense of warmth to a predominantly cool scheme.

ABOVE: Mingling reds and pinks calls for considerable skill if the result is not to set the teeth on edge. At Frith Lodge, Sussex, this has been successfully accomplished by surrounding salmon-pink and vermilion oriental poppies, magenta cistus and rosy-mauve lupins and foxgloves with the emollient tones of ivory roses, lime-yellow lady's mantle and blue-violet geraniums. The staddle stones set in silvery stachys are ice cool to the eye before the joyous burst of colour that lies beyond them.

RIGHT: Blue and yellow are a classic combination, even though pairing strong yellow and deep blue is risky. But with the leaven of plenty of green and softer yellows, and under the rain-washed skies of Scotland it works well, the blues almost thunderous, the yellows lively rather than brash. These borders at House of Pitmuies, Angus, are typical of the English style, for all that they are in Scotland. The same cool, wet climate, and similar plantings, can also be seen in the north-west of England.

FAR RIGHT, ABOVE: Another expression of blue with yellow, at Wallington, Northumberland, with a blue clematis spanning, like the arch of the heavens, a path flanked by borders with 'golden' foliage – more lime green than yellow in this northerly garden – and incidents of yellow and blue flowers.

RIGHT: After the sober face of Powis Castle seen on page 24, this planting is an example of the skill with which colour and form of flower and leaf are blended in the terrace borders. The components of this scene are primrose-yellow achillea, rich blue agapanthus, the acid yellow of a tall spurge, and a violet-blue clematis opening from silvery buds, all backed by a smoky blue ceanothus. Before long the ivory wands of a cimicifuga will open to add a contrasting outline to the picture.

opium poppies, in which the seedheads that follow are also globular. Other flowers that, like peonies, make their impact as much or more in the form of the individual flower than in the mass are irises, lilies, daylilies, arum lilies, and even certain daisies: those that, like rudbeckias and *Echinacea*, have a bold central cone of green or black or tan.

Though cited for their flower form, several of these plants have handsome leaves, and leaves, of course, last longer than flowers and are correspondingly more significant as elements in the border when outline and form are in question. To the dew-capturing, scalloped fans of *Alchemilla mollis* and the glaucous spears of bearded irises, the pleated broadswords of crocosmia, the ferny foliage of astilbes, often richly-coloured in spring, the dissected,

RIGHT:
Powis Castle's terrace borders in fiery mode, with scarlet rose hips, a bright red crocosmia and another in burnt orange, refulgent against the violet-purple of a lobelia and, on the wall, magenta-purple *Clematis viticella* 'Purpurea Plena Elegans', and the lemon yellow, black-eyed daisies of rudbeckia, prefiguring the silver, lemon and white grouping further from the eye. The combination of hardy and tender perennials, for which Powis is renowned, is increasingly popular in English gardens.

ABOVE:
Strong contrasts at Powis Castle, with vermilion *Crocosmia* 'Lucifer', its bold sword leaves almost as striking as its flowers, against a backdrop of sultry blue-violet monkshoods, with their curious, almost sinister, hooded flowers and deeply dissected foliage.

dark leaves of monkshoods, the arching blades of daylilies, the bloomy fleshiness of sedums, or the bold, deeply-cut leaves of acanthus, one may add a great many border plants chosen especially for their foliage. There are hostas, of course, and bergenias, for broad, substantial leaves; ferns for filigree and lace; grasses for the fountain-like elegance of their arching blades; yuccas with stiffly upright or arching spears in rosette formation and phormiums likewise, but with their blades arranged in fans.

When it comes to texture, again there is an extraordinary diversity to choose from. Visual texture and tactile may be at odds with each other – a mass of small leaves giving a soft or feathery visual texture may be hard and spiky to the touch, as in some junipers, for example. Both kinds of texture are

LEFT: The execution at Stobshiel, East Lothian, is very different from the rose garden at Sissinghurst, but the principle is similar: the formlessness and profusion of old roses is constrained by a strong, clean-cut design of clipped hedge and wall. Beyond the broad, square battlements of the main dividing hedge is a glimpse, between ancient yews, of borrowed Elysian landscape, where sheep graze on sun-warmed grass. The sculpture at the centre of the little lawn is by Elizabeth Frink.

ABOVE: At Powis Castle a bower of mingled violet and pink clematis, rounded in outline to echo the rounded faces of the clematis themselves, is set amidst a mixture of lemon and white so airy it could be about to take flight: the lemon-green fuzz of *Thalictrum flavum glaucum*, a form of meadow rue, and narrow spires of snowy white cimicifugas, their slender candles echoed by the rich magenta of purple loosestrife. Echoing the violet clematis is a good, dark form of summer-flowering ceanothus, given substance by the bloomy, dark sword leaves of New Zealand flax (*Phormium tenax*).

significant in the border, especially if you are the touchy-feely sort who loves to stroke the woolly softness of lambs' ears (*Stachys byzantina*), gently rub between finger and thumb the figured-velvet of *Geranium renardii*, or run a hand over a silken ripple of *Artemisia schmidtiana* 'Nana'. With these, we move into the realm of foliage colour, for many plants with a strong tactile appeal are endowed with a coat of white hairs or dense felting which gives them their silvery or platinum or pewter colouring. The waxen or grape-like bloom on other plants – rue, blue hostas, seakale – gives them a glaucous, blue-grey cast. Then there are green-leaved plants with leathery, or glittering, or softly matt surfaces, all of which vary the textures in the border.

The border may also include evergreen shrubs: small hebes in apple-green or pewter-grey; silvery, misty grey or vivid green santolinas; the delightfully obese *Ozothamnus ledifolius* with its resinous, yellow-backed needle leaves and russet flower-buds; *Salvia officinalis* 'Purpurascens' with soft grey-purple foliage; the very dark green *Iberis sempervirens*. Then there are many taller evergreens that could be included to lend substance to the planting, such as Mexican orange (*Choisya ternata*), mahonias, holly in its many variants, and *Phillyrea*. All these help to clothe the border in winter.

This leads to a consideration of the types of plants that might accompany the classic border perennials. There is a range of soft-wooded, summer-flowering shrubs particularly well suited to mixed borders. Though somewhat formless, many of them can be cut hard back in spring to flower abundantly and long on the new season's growths. Among them are caryopteris, with its turpentine-aromatic, grey foliage and fuzzy violet-blue flowers followed by verdigris-blue seed heads; fuchsias in great variety; and the pink haze of summer-flowering tamarisks; ceratostigmas, valued for their rich ultramarine-blue flowers and crimson autumn tints; indigoferas with their dainty pink or lilac pea-flowers; yellow-cupped *Hypericum* 'Hidcote'; the coconut-scented Spanish broom (*Spartium junceum*), which responds well to annual stooling; and cape figworts (*Phygelius*), with sprays of curving trumpets in clear scarlet, coral or primrose.

Yet another class of shrubs for the border are the

old domesticated, summer-flowering kinds like mock orange, weigela, deutzia, and for later in the season the mop-headed hydrangeas in pink or blue (according to soil) and white, or the forms of *Hydrangea paniculata* with their lacy or sterile pyramid heads of white flowers. In their season they are full of flower, and the mock oranges fill the garden with scent. They are especially valuable where a mixed border includes old shrub roses, for many of them date from the same period, the nineteenth century, and appear comfortably at ease with the roses and each other. Buddlejas are a later arrival, but also look well in the mixed border, and can be

cut back to a low framework of branches to keep them compact and full of their honey-scented flower-spikes.

Ornamental grasses are of great value in the border, with their graceful blades; and many of them have beautiful inflorescences as well, the plumes of pampas of course, but also the rippling, silken tresses of *Miscanthus sinensis*, the airy fountain of the giant oat (*Stipa gigantea*) or the softly-tinted, furry caterpillars of *Pennisetum* species. Bulbs can be tucked in among clumps of perennials or beneath shrubs, to flower early in the year before the border has woken up. Chionodoxas and scillas, for example, will seed

LEFT: The play of light, as much as its quality, affects our perception of colour and form. In this green and yellow border at Hadspen Garden, Somerset, the great velvety leaves of a coppiced paulownia, in the left foreground, are thrown into relief by the light reflected from the surface of the upper leaves, while those beneath are backlit and translucent green. The tall fountain of grass beyond is golden in the sunlight, and its colouring is echoed by the clear yellow daisies of *Senecio* 'Sunshine' at its feet, by yellow mulleins and achilleas, and by the creamy-gold foliage of *Lonicera nitida* 'Baggesen's Gold' in the foreground. The whole scene is bathed in light, and the purple-leaved filbert in the background seems all the darker as a result, yet gleaming where the sun's rays touch it.

ABOVE: An all-green planting allows for contrasts in texture and tone to be given full value, in this corner of a border at Sticky Wicket, Dorset. The chartreuse foam of lady's mantle (*Alchemilla mollis*) is set off by its own rounded, soft almond-green foliage, against which the small leaves of cotoneasters, above and below, etch a dark pattern. The clipped box globe in its wooden tub plays with the notion of roundness that finds leafy expression in the lady's mantle.

themselves to make a brilliant carpet of azure in earliest spring, pale daffodils are exquisite among the richly-tinted new growths of herbaceous peonies, and tulips arise stately and elegant from among the unfurling green foliage of geraniums or the fingered foliage of lupins.

Biennials such as foxgloves, stocks, sweet williams and evening primroses, add summer colour, and for spring there are other biennials, notably honesty (*Lunaria annua*) and forget-me-nots. The first should be left to produce their glistening ivory honesty 'money' in autumn as the seeds (that will produce the next generation of spring flower) ripen and fall; forget-me-nots can be simply torn out in handfuls

ABOVE: Beyond this border at Barnsley House, Gloucestershire, are the cylindrical yews that flank the rock-rose path (see page 30), lending a note of mock solemnity to the soft outlines of the flower border. Blue campanulas and white anaphalis pick up the sombre purple and ivory of acanthus spires and, beyond them, the cool grey stone of the house, while fiery tones of crocosmia, to the right and Peruvian lily (*Alstroemeria aurea*), to the left, frame the picture.

ABOVE RIGHT: Tightly corseted against the onset of middle-aged spread, the Barnsley yews are frost-topped in this autumn scene. The acanthus spikes have turned to brown, and the crocosmia is now in seed, its sword leaves contrasting with the leathery paddles of bergenia. Pink dendranthemas and deeper, dusty pink sedum remind us that autumn need not be a season only of the scarlet and gold of falling leaves.

as they fade, at the moment when spring yields to summer. Annuals for the border range from substantial plants such as the castor oil plant for bold foliage, the massive, deliciously night-scented *Nicotiana sylvestris*, burnt-orange *Tithonia rotundifolia* and spidery cleomes in pink or white, through *Cosmos bipinnatus* (also in pink or white, with lacy foliage), the daintier *Nicotiana langsdorfii* with its tiny lime-green, blue-eyelashed trumpets in airy sprays, *Lavatera trimestris*, which comes in rose, pink or pure white, and the related *Malope trifida* in glowing rose-red, to *Cuphea miniata* 'Firefly' in vivid carmine, azure-blue love-in-a-mist and gentian-blue *Anagallis linifolia*, lemon yellow *Calceolaria mexicana* which

bears masses of little slipper flowers, and much more besides. The seed lists are a winter delight for the border planner and a matchless resource if there are gaps to be filled in an established border.

The other group of plants that lend themselves to 'in-and-out' gardening are tender perennials, many of which flower for weeks or even months on end or have handsome foliage. As Miss Jekyll well knew, they also bring colours that are scarce among hardy perennials, such as the strong, pure reds. Over the last decade or so tender perennials have become much more popular in English gardens, and can be found adding colour and form to many a summer border. As well as such old favourites as dahlias and the pure blue *Salvia patens*, there are verbenas in pink, crimson, magenta and scarlet; large-belled bedding penstemons in a range of jewel colours; Paris daisies in white, pink, peach and shades of yellow, and the lovely glaucous-blue, filigree-leaved *Argyranthemum foeniculaceum* with pure white daisies; osteospermums both spreading and upright, with white, inky-blue backed, pink, purple or buff-yellow daisies; cannas with their great paddle leaves in green or bloomy purple; silvery, comb-like *Senecio vira-vira*, and trailing *Helichrysum petiolare*, its heart-shaped, felted leaves typically grey but also available variegated cream on grey or in the luminous chartreuse yellow of 'Limelight'. Both the senecio and the helichrysum have the invaluable quality of interweaving with their neighbours without choking them, so you can contrive, as does Christopher Lloyd in his Long Border at Great Dixter, to have the rich scarlet spikes and beetroot-purple leaves of *Lobelia* 'Queen Victoria' wreathed in the silver of the senecio, or mingle *Helichrysum petiolare* 'Limelight' with the lax, spreading arms set with finely dissected green foliage and lemon yellow lazy-daisies of *Bidens ferulifolia*, another tender perennial that flowers all summer.

And what of the arrangement of the plants within the border? The old way was to bank them more or less evenly for height, low plants at the front, tallest at the back. But this can be monotonous, and an unnecessary constraint. In many of the most satisfying borders, tall but see-through plants, such as the sparsely-leaved *Verbena bonariensis* with its thin, angular stems topped by rich violet-purple heads, are placed at or near the front of the border where you may enjoy at close quarters the extraordinary colour-changes that come over the flowers at dusk, as well as their sweet fragrance. Viewed front on, a border with dips and peaks is more appealing than one which has a row of plants at the back of more or less uniform height. Then, too, there are tall plants which have poise and beauty from head to toe, and which deserve to be seen in their entirety: such are the plume poppy (*Macleaya microcarpa*), with its bold, glaucous-grey, white-backed leaves all the way up the stem and tall plumes of tiny coral buds opening to fawn-pink stars; *Selinum wallichianum*, a Queen Anne's lace of extreme refinement with a

BELOW: Tidy gardeners who cut everything down in autumn might not see the point of this winter border at Waterperry Gardens, Oxfordshire; but this scene of parchment-pale and amber and tan foliage, all touched to silver by the frost, has its own tousled, chilly charm.

RIGHT: Autumn has passed into winter, leaving this private garden in Hereford and Worcester frosted to monochrome simplicity; only shapes, and the long shadows of sentinel conifers across the whitened lawn, remain.

pile of finely dissected green foliage beneath a wide white umbel held on ivory-white spokes; and some verbascums, with broad, silver-felted basal leaves and white-woolly flower spikes from which emerge clear yellow flowers.

With so much richness to choose from, the successful borders are invariably those where aesthetic considerations dominate; where the constraints of a careful scheme – whether based on colour, texture or form, whether intended to stimulate through the use of contrast or suggest repose with soothing harmonies – have exercised a discipline on the plant-lover's desire to enjoy the individual beauties of more and more plants, subsuming the collector's instinct to the artistic impulse.

SYMPHONIC PLANTINGS

THE GHOSTLY
LINGERING EFFECT OF WHITE FLOWERS IN DEEP SHADE
OR AT NIGHTFALL IS WELL KNOWN. LESS OFTEN
REMARKED UPON IS THE QUALITY OF CERTAIN PINK,
ROSE-PURPLE AND VIOLET TONES TO CHANGE WITH THE
LIGHT, FROM VIVIDLY WARM IN THE SUN TO COOL IN
THE SHADE – YET BY SOME PARADOX TO BE BRIEFLY
FLATTERED BY THE FADING LIGHT TO GLOWING
WARMTH. THE CRIMSON-PURPLE OF FOXGLOVES, LIT BY
THE EVENING SUN, JUMPS TO THE EYE FROM AMONG
THIS COOL PLANTING OF TENDER BLUES AND WHITE,
WITH PALE LEMON LUPINS, AT THE MENAGERIE,
NORTHAMPTONSHIRE.

Some gardeners say that Nature's colours never clash. As Vita Sackville-West, whose ability to handle colours with sensitivity is so evident at Sissinghurst, once observed: 'Whoever it was who said Nature made no mistake in colour-harmony was either colour-blind or a sentimentalist'. The colours of flowers evolved to attract pollinators, whose eyes see very differently from ours; and though it is not a necessary corollary that to our eyes Nature's colours may quarrel, they can and sometimes do. As Vita Sackville-West continued:

LEFT: The enduring popularity of blue, yellow and white is evident in this planting at Sticky Wicket, Dorset, where violet-blue is used in a subordinate role to an abundance of clear yellow and white. Contrasts of form are discreetly used to effect too: the spires of blue lupins emphasizing the flat plates of achilleas in canary yellow and cream.

RIGHT: Another yellow, white and blue planting, this time at The Garden House, Buckland Monachorum, Devon, contrasts the violet-blue, ivory and alabaster spires of camassias with the strong mounded outline of white broom and yellow rhododendrons.

'Nature sometimes makes the most hideous mistakes; and it is up to us gardeners to control and correct them.' Once the plant breeders began to lend a hand to evolution, raising ever bigger and brighter bedding plants – a trend that began in the nineteenth century with the advent of plate glass and thus the greenhouse, coinciding with the availability of cheap labour and fuel for heating – the scope for painful clashes became all the greater.

Miss Jekyll's influence, however, and that of her disciples and successors, has been immeasurable; in garden after English garden, one may see colour used with skill and subtlety in borders of one colour of a restricted palette. Often a leaven of sharply

contrasting or vivid tones, used with restraint, adds sparkle to an otherwise subdued planting where pastel shades alone would lack vitality: acid yellow with peachy pinks, or scarlet with mauve and purple amid grey foliage. An all-white planting may be alluringly ghostly, as at Sissinghurst (see page 12), or vibrant and emphatic if touches of bright colour are used to illuminate the white (see page 95). Form and texture add a further dimension to the plant groupings that have lasting appeal.

Small children are attracted by bright, primary colours, but as we grow up our eye becomes more or less attuned to subtlety of colour, alone and in combination. We can, of course, consciously educate ourselves to see, rather than letting colour merely bounce off the unselective retina; and in the business of colour planning, the now-familiar colour wheel is a useful aid to education. Picture the primary colours (red, blue, yellow) disposed evenly around a circle linked by their intermediates (purple, orange, green), and draw a line across its diameter, joining the complementary colours of red and green, so as to divide the circle into two halves. Where red is the pivot, the other two primary colours impart their character each to one of the

halves. The yellow range – vermilion and orange-red through to yellow-green – faces the blue range which includes blue-green through to red-purple and crimson. Put at its simplest, clashes are avoided by keeping yellow-based reds and pinks away from those which fall into the blue half of the spectrum.

The quality and intensity of light affect the way we see colours, as well as the immediate context. A Mediterranean landscape in high summer appears bleached to a uniform yet brilliant, warm white by the intensity of the sun striking on stone and earth, so that only vivid colours retain any individuality. Conversely, under the grey-blue light of an English sky these same bright colours may seem garish; but pastel tones come into their own. Deep colours absorb more light than pale ones; white, and the very palest blues, lilacs and creams, show up best at dusk or in deep shadow, for they reflect almost all the available light. Whenever visiting hours allow, it is worth seeing gardens in the early morning or

ABOVE: At Sticky Wicket, Dorset, a group of strong magentas, crimsons and purples – columbines and alliums and geraniums – assertive enough to hold their own against the thrusting sword leaves of bearded iris at the centre. The flowers of the iris themselves are in the same potent purple, with velvety falls and paler standards translucent in the low rays of the sun.

RIGHT: Still at Sticky Wicket, pink mallow, cosmos and lupins and purple-leaved red orach in the foreground are set against a tapestry backdrop in shades of purple and violet and grey, enlivened by acid and primrose yellow. These sharp or tender tones of yellow are as easy to place, as flattering to their companions of any colour, as the brasher brassy or mustard yellows are quarrelsome.

LEFT: Pink, purple and lavender tones in a private garden in Northamptonshire designed by Dan Pearson. The dusty grey-purple of *Salvia officinalis* 'Purpurascens', a form of the culinary sage, is a gentle accompaniment to bright pink roses, and is echoed by the feathery haze of purple fennel and the more intense, metallic purple-maroon of purple filbert and purple smoke bush (*Cotinus coggygria*). The leaven, here, is the inclusion of poppies: a strong group in white with striking black eyes, and a sprinkling of watermelon-pink.

evening hours, when the sun is low and the play of light and shadow greatly enhances the subtlety of colour that characterizes the best of English garden planting (see pages 60–1).

In English gardens, thanks to the country's temperate climate, colours are almost always seen in a context of the greens of foliage and grass. Leaves come in an immense range of greens – pale almond green, fresh apple green and sharp lime and chartreuse, grey-green, olive green, sea green and glaucous and dark, glittering greens – to say nothing of grey and silver, purple and bronze and copper, and variegated foliage.

Appreciating harmonious colour schemes, then, is more than just associating the right flowers; it

ABOVE: In the same Northamptonshire garden is another group of pink flowers – the candy pink pokers of *Persicaria bistorta* 'Superba', flat heads of pink cow parsley, chalky-pink flowers of *Geranium macrorrhizum* – with white bleeding heart (*Dicentra spectabilis alba*) and a purple filbert, its young growths glowing like garnets in the spring sun.

LEFT: At Herterton House, Northumberland, paving is invaded and overlaid by small carpeting plants, with taller incidents: the double columbine (*Aquilegia* 'Nora Barlow') in terracotta-pink and green, soft orange poppies (*Papaver atlanticum*), white irises, pink bistort among them.

ABOVE RIGHT: In a small garden the choice may lie between rigorous discipline, or happy abandon – the course chosen here, at Beechcroft Road in Oxford, where a narrow paved path winds between flowers and shrubs so closely packed that even the most persistent weed might despair of gaining roothold. Multi-layered plantings, with perennials between and below the shrubs and trees, and climbers scrambling through the branches, makes the best possible use of space; and if bulbs are planted among the perennials, there can be early and late colour as well.

calls for sensitivity to foliage as well. A symphonic planting in the blue range, which may include true blue and the gamut of 'nurserymen's blue – the range of colours often called blue in catalogues, but which runs from greyish lavender almost to pinky mauve – as well as violet, purple, magenta, crimson and blue-pinks, will be enhanced by grey, silver and glaucous foliage and the bluer greens, with purple-leaved plants for the deeper bass notes (see the endpapers, and pages 88–9). Used with discretion, touches of contrasting colour – in this case, cream or primrose or pale lemon with the purer blues, or soft pure scarlet with the violets and purples – will heighten the impression of blueness.

In the yellow range, from cream and all the shades of yellow through to orange and the pale tints of peach and apricot and buff, we can choose from lime-yellow foliage and the sharper, fresher greens, as well as bronze and coppery foliage (see page 78). With a restricted palette, avoid anything redder than ochre or mustard yellow; chartreuse and fresh green foliage alone is the most satisfactory. Again, the sense of yellowness can be heightened by touches of the complementary colour – in this case, violet-blue (complementary colours are those that face each other on the colour wheel: red and green, yellow and violet, orange and blue). To accompany the warmer, softer shades of cream, buff and apricot, choose bronze and coppery foliage; with the sharper orange and vermilion, both coppery foliage and acid green, separately or in combination, look well (see pages 18 and 59).

Some colours, notably all the strong reds from magenta to vermilion-orange, appear to advance to meet the eye. By contrast blue, violet and blue-mauve are known as recessive colours, because they give an impression of being further from the observer than they really are. The trick of creating a false sense of distance by planting a drift of soft, smoky blue flowers is well known. It is perhaps less obvious

that a blob of bright scarlet or magenta at the far end of a vista will have the effect of seeming to fore-shorten the perspective. Strong and recessive colours together can be tricky, too. A combination of deep strong colours and pale recessive ones will heighten still more the impact of the deeper colour; for example, velvety dark red roses rising from a cloud of the lacy, pale lavender-flowered *Hebe* 'Bowles' Variety'.

There is a particular difficulty with the colours described as pink, which can range from mauve and light purple through sugar pink to coral and salmon. The mauve-pink of many heathers, splen-did under the rain-washed skies of a Scottish moor-land, swears abominably with the orange-russet foliage of certain *Calluna* cultivars; the rather harsh,

bluish candy pink of some flowering cherries assorts disastrously with their unfurling coppery young leaves. The early-flowering cherry 'Okame', seen in isolation, seems to be burdened with blossom of the same rather unappealing pink; but set it in a patch of muddy mauve-pink *Erica* x *darleyensis* 'Cherry Stevens', and the cherry appears as clear pink, the heather a striking, thunderous purple. The bigger Japanese cherries with pink flowers are best seen against a backdrop of the bluish-green foliage of conifers, or the purple haze of distant birches.

Magenta is a colour that belongs in this range, and at its best it is a fine, strong crimson with a good deal of blue in it, redder, cleaner and more astrin-gent than purple. It occurs in certain cistus, in *Rosa rugosa*, and in some hardy geraniums. To play safe it

ABOVE: 'Brightly coloured hay', in the phrase of garden designer Russell Page; but charming with it. In fact, these are cornfield rather than hayfield flowers: red poppies and yellow corn marigolds, evenly scattered with blue cornflowers and pink corn cockles, in a seed mixture supplied by Miriam Rothschild and described by her as 'Farmer's Nightmare'. They make this flowery meadow strip at Chatsworth, Derbyshire, vivid but not garish.

ABOVE: Massed white marguerites almost conceal the wooden seat, bleached to silvery-grey by the sun, standing against a stone wall in this private garden in Northamptonshire designed by Dan Pearson. The scarlet of poppies serves to heighten the effect of the white daisies.

can be associated with grey and silver foliage; more imaginatively, it is flattered by cream, primrose and soft lemon. The least satisfactory accompaniment to the purple-magenta-mauve range of colours is the strong green of grass and other mid-green foliage; blue- and grey-greens, smoky purple and glaucous foliage and grey stone are a better choice. Touches of chartreuse, on the other hand, can deliciously enliven the quieter pinks and purples. *Alchemilla mollis* is a constant favourite as a companion for old roses, on account of its lime-yellow froth of flower, and an airy spurge can be used with discretion in among a purple patch of *Rosa glauca*, *Fuchsia* 'Mrs Popple' and *Clematis* 'Abundance'.

And what of white? Although white might seem to be the absence of colour, non-colour, it can be remarkably insistent. It clashes with nothing. In the Jekyll canon, white assorts most happily of all with blue, or with rose pink, or with deep yellow, but least agreeably with bright green, violet or orange. Miss Jekyll liked to use harmonies of pure colour, tint and white – pure blue, pale blue and white, for example. White alone can be very effective, giving scope for exploiting the innumerable nuances of white – snow, chalk, milk, ivory, cream, alabaster, pearl – and textures from waxen and crystalline to froth and foam, heightened perhaps by platinum and pewter foliage or (as at Sissinghurst) framed in dark green. And just as touches of white can add sparkle to a border of mixed colour, so flashes of a bright colour, such as scarlet or candy-pink, can make a drift of white flowers seem whiter still.

WATER IN
THE GARDEN

O NATIVE ENGLISH

POOL BENEATH SHADY WILLOWS OR BUBBLING CHALK

STREAM, THOUGH IT MIGHT BE MARGINED WITH

YELLOW FLAGS OR MARSH MARIGOLDS, EVER BOASTED

CANDELABRA PRIMULAS, HOSTAS, AND ARUM LILIES. AS

WITH WOODLAND, SO WITH WATER, THE ENGLISH SEEK

EFFECTS THAT NATURE MIGHT HAVE ACHIEVED HAD SHE

HAD HER WITS ABOUT HER. WATER IS THE ALLY OF THIS

PASSION FOR PLANTS IN COOL, LUSH GROUPINGS OF

EXOTICS LIKE THIS STREAMSIDE PLANTING IN

A PRIVATE GARDEN IN DEVON.

LEFT: At Knightshayes Court, Devon, the garden is characterized by restrained formality near the house, passing into a paradise woodland that merges into the distant landscape. This simple, circular pool, surrounded by grass and square-clipped yew hedges, is watched over by a weeping silver pear. White, crimson and pink water lilies, and water irises in blue and white, grow in the pool but most of the surface is kept clear, reflecting the sky in all its changing moods.

Water has countless moods and expressions. It can be violent and destructive, as it falls in torrents down a mountainside or bursts the banks of a river to flood low-lying plains. But it also, when captured and still in a pool or canal, speaks of tranquillity and peace. Persuaded to flow in channels and over small falls, it sings, and its sound soothes and consoles, just as the sound of small waves lapping the shore is a lullaby. The squeak of a hand-operated pump or a well-chain speaks not only of the hard work in earning a drink, but also of the mystery of water: Saint Exupéry's *'chant de l'eau et toutes ses musiques criardes'*. Water is a willing accomplice in practical jokes and illusion: the fountain that spurts water on the unwary passer-by, the dark pool that mirrors its surroundings. All these qualities, even its irrepressible nature, can be evoked in a garden. Even its functionality can be given aesthetic meaning. In hot climates moving water, flowing through marble halls or playing as fountains, acts as a natural air condi-

tioner, cooling the atmosphere. A dipping tank, from which water is drawn for flagging plants, can be visually compelling as well as useful. In the garden where I was brought up, just such a dipping tank still stands, surrounded by ferns, stately irises, tall, fragrant Himalayan cowslips and the rounded, scalloped leaves of *Darmera peltata*, which bears heads of pale pink flowers on naked stems in early spring, even before the fern croziers have unfurled. Wherever there is water in the garden, formal or seemingly natural, its life-giving qualities always inform our response to its presence.

This fascination with water as more than merely the basis of life is age-old. Pliny the Younger, whom we met in Chapter 2 as an enthusiast for topiary, also described the fountains, basins, rills and rivulets of his Umbrian garden. Even earlier, in biblical times, Solomon's Song of Songs sings of the beauty of flowers and trees, in 'a garden enclosed – a garden of living waters, and flowing streams from Lebanon'. The Europe of the Dark Ages, however,

RIGHT: The same circular pool at Knightshayes is here revealed in its wooded setting, from which perfectly manicured yew hedges separate it. This time it is not the sky which is mirrored, but the blue *Iris ensata* and the ghostly reflection of a white-flowered dogwood tree beyond the hedge, shimmering in the mysterious, dark depths of the water.

LEFT: Irises and water lilies again, but this is a formal pool in a different, more domestic mood, at Tintinhull House, Somerset. Yellow flags (*Iris pseudacorus*) decorate the four corners of the rectangular pool. Again, much of the surface of the water is kept clear, to reflect the irises, and the pillars of the classically simple sitting place beyond. One is reminded of Pliny's open-air dining arbour, with its four marble columns and stone water basin.

ABOVE: A view from the sitting place itself at Tintinhull, with urns of white Paris daisies and crimson flax (*Linum grandiflorum* 'Rubrum') echoing the creamy-primrose and crimson water lilies.

dominated by the other-worldliness, the rejection of sensual pleasure that typified Christian belief, had no interest in the garden as art, but thought of a horticulture above all as utilitarian, and the garden as a place to grow vegetables, fruit and culinary and medicinal herbs, where water was merely the necessary element to growth.

Larger houses and monasteries would also have one or more stew-ponds, where fish were kept, to be easily accessible for the meatless Friday or Lent table. Some of these stew-ponds survive to this day, though their functional role has long vanished.

Where there was a reliable and sufficient source, water served, too, to power the mills that ground corn for the coarse bread of the times, and a few water mills, complete with wheel and mill-race where the water was channelled to maximum velocity, can still be seen; elsewhere, mill-ponds and leats (the open water-courses that guide the stream to the waterwheel) have, like the surviving stew-ponds, been made into elements of the pleasure garden, with decorative golden orfe or koi carp, perhaps, in place of the fish that in medieval times would have been destined for the table. Here and there survives, too, the wide and deep, water-filled moats that surrounded fortified manor houses and castles to protect them from attack, until growing political stability made such defences unnecessary.

It remained to other civilizations, that were later to become the inspiration and the artistic and intellectual resource of the European Renaissance, to maintain the garden as an aesthetic and, above all,

a religious and spiritual experience during the time of Europe's retreat into the denial of sensuous pleasures. The builders of the paradise gardens of Zoroastrian Persia, and the later Islamic gardens of Persia, India and Spain that they inspired, created gardens as places of beauty, where the soul might find tranquillity and the mind repose from the struggle to survive in harsh, arid climates. In these gardens, arising from the same impulse as those the Song of Songs extols, water played a central role.

ABOVE: The long, narrow pool at York Gate, Yorkshire, is unusual in being raised, so the water is at waist height, with a broad stone surround on three sides inviting one to sit and trail a hand in the water, and a round-topped wall on the fourth. One end is clear of water lilies, to allow the fountain to pattern the surface of the water with droplets and fill the air with sound.

LEFT: In this private garden in Shropshire, planted by Mirabel Osler, a diversity of plants surround the pool: ferns, irises, yellow loosestrife, and pale yellow primulas, with lady's mantle and a deep crimson rose which looks across the water to the climbing roses on the old stone walls.

ABOVE: The Siberian iris, *Iris sibirica*, will grow equally well in ordinary border soil or at the stream- or pool-side, where its graceful flights of flower, poised above sword leaves, are in perfect harmony with the mood of water both still and moving. Here they grow in a lush, leafy planting at Rosemoor Garden, Devon.

LEFT: Although its setting, at Shute House, Dorset, is the green lawns and lush plantings of an English garden designed by Sir Geoffrey Jellicoe, this deceptively simple rill, with its cascades and square pools, has evident links with the irrigation channels of the Middle East which were the inspiration for the watercourses of the Persian paradise garden and the Islamic gardens that, in turn, drew upon the symbolism of the Persian garden and linked it with the symbols of the Qur'anic heaven, a place of shady trees beneath which rivers flow. In arid climates, water is self-evidently the symbol and basis of life; in climates where water is taken almost for granted, it still has a profound spiritual and emotional effect in the garden, which at Shute is developed to a high degree in the musicality of the successive cascades.

Indispensable to very existence itself, water came to symbolize life both physical and spiritual, and the design of the gardens was based on an idealized pattern of irrigation channels, walled to protect the precious oasis elements of water and shade-giving trees from the dust and scorching wind of the desert. Fountains added their music and cooled the air. The great Mughal gardens, the Shalimar Bagh in Lahore and the summer gardens of Kashmir, were graced by elegant pavilions, often entirely surrounded by water in which fountains played. To these pavilions the ruler and his court would repair at night, to enjoy the cooling air and the reflections of the moon in the water. The rill, a narrow, usually stone-bordered channel much used by Sir Edwin

ABOVE: Whereas the water at Shute seen from below is full of movement and vitality as well as music, from above it appears more static, its downward impulse interrupted by the horizontals of the crossing slabs and pools. The lush planting of the upper levels – the big paddle leaves of bog arums, blades of hostas, the creamy foam of *Aruncus* – gives way to smooth grass around the pools.

105

Lutyens in his garden designs (as at Hestercombe, see page 9), is clearly derived from the irrigation channels of the paradise garden, though in Lutyens' hands it has come to be seen as quintessentially of the English Edwardian garden style, and it has been stripped of its religious symbolism to become a purely decorative element.

LEFT: The broad, tranquil expanse of water at Vann, Surrey, gives almost the feeling of security of a moated manor. The waterside planting is kept extremely simple, with grass right to the water's edge varied by clumps of the sword leaves of irises, leaving little to distract the eye from the reflections of sky and tree-trunk and leafy canopy.

RIGHT: Water has many moods; the pool at Vann, hazy in the light of a spring dawn, evokes a kind of cool detachment that is not quite tranquillity, and is very different from the revivifying quality of moving water sparkling in the sunlight. The white snowballs of the guelder rose (*Viburnum opulus* 'Roseum'), arching over unfurling *Gunnera* leaves in the foreground, are in perfect harmony with the quiet, misty water.

Even in gentler climates like that of Britain, washed by the rain-laden winds of the Gulf Stream, this sense of water as the very stuff of life remains, however, responding to something deep in the human psyche where age-old memories and symbols reside. From the great landscape gardens of eighteenth-century England, such as Stourhead (see page 33) in which whole valleys were submerged to create lakes spanned by graceful bridges, to the smallest of front garden rockeries into which the proud owner has shoehorned a tiny preformed

pond and pump-driven fountain, water – moving or still, naturalistic or frankly artificial – is an essential aesthetic as well as functional element in European gardens. Only in Victorian England, it seems, did water cease to be valued as an element of design; though the Victorians' taste for bibelots and knick-knacks, evident in their cluttered houses, seems to have extended to their gardens too and to have included, at worst, such niaiseries as mock well-heads and bridges that led over nothing to nowhere amid 'jam-tart' beds of annuals.

The nineteenth century was a time when countless new plants were introduced to Britain. The era of the plant-lover was born. For the artist-plantsman, and above all for the plant collector, water in the garden is a means of greatly extending the

ABOVE: Natural streams and pools may be alive with light or dark with mystery, but the frankly artificial blue of a swimming pool is usually an eyesore in the garden. Here just such a turquoise-lined pool has been turned into part of the experience of the garden, narrowly framed in stone, its extreme horizontality massively emphasized by the clipped yew hedge with its bulky central arch and the squat pillars and domes of yew beyond. The hedges were there before the pool was conceived, and dictated its form, down to the swimming 'tunnel' to the second pool beyond.

range of plants that will grow successfully. Candelabra primulas, some of the finest irises and ferns, globe flowers, foamy meadowsweets, ligularias with their bold leaves and great heads of golden, butterfly-thralling daisies, scarlet lobelias, feathery astilbes, purple loosestrife, graceful sedges, arum lilies, web-footed or horse-chestnut-leaved rodgersias, and the monumental gunnera – all these thrive in damp soil, while in the water itself, water lilies float waxen on the surface amid their flat, circular pads. Though lush water-side plantings have their own charm, the temptation to overplant must be resisted if the delight of the water itself is not to be lost; changes of pace from jungle luxuriance to the bare water itself, grassy-banked or stone-edged, give full value to both the plants and the water.

Even a trickling brook has its own charm, let alone a rushing cascade or a pool in which the song of the water is momentarily silenced to be replaced by the poetry of mirrored reflections.

For reflections to be given their full aesthetic value, in which the symbolism of their evanescence can be most fully experienced, the water should be kept as high as possible relative to the paving or grass which surrounds the pool; and this is equally true of an informal pool as of a formal *bassin* or *pièce d'eau*. A pool intended for reflections, furthermore, should have expanses of water free of the distractions of water lilies or other aquatic plants, nor should the surface of the water be broken up by the falling drops of a fountain. To have both the tranquillity of water-mirrored images and the music of

ABOVE: The Stobo Water Garden in Tweeddale has a Chinese flavour, with its bridge arching over and reflected in a tree-shaded pool, and framing a shallow, rocky cascade. Where moving and still water alternate, reflections, and especially those of a static object such as this bridge, take on an added dimension by emphasizing the change to tranquillity.

water alive with movement needs careful management, or ample space (as at Shute, see page 104–5).

Water in movement, in the form of cascades and waterfalls, was a feature of Roman gardens, and these purely sensuous delights reappear in the great Italian formal gardens of the later Renaissance, along with fountains decorated with elaborate statuary. The emphasis on greenery, shade and water, stonework and marble, which we find in Pliny's descriptions, remained characteristic of Italian gardens. Perhaps the most famous are the gardens of the Villa d'Este, at Tivoli, where a dazzling succession of waterfalls and fountains fills the air with the constant thunder and splashing of water.

French and Dutch gardens of the period, by contrast, often featured the still waters of a canal, of which the grandest examples are the Grand Canal at Fontainebleau, built for François I, and the great *allées d'eaux* of Le Nôtre at Vaux-le-Vicomte and Versailles. A miniature version survives in the Dutch garden at Westbury-on-Severn, Gloucestershire, but the pool and pavilion of Tintinhull (see page 100) looks back, rather, to the classical era; it is possible to imagine oneself in the garden of a villa

in Roman Britain. Turning their backs on formality, the English designers of the eighteenth century used large expanses of water as an element in their idealized, romanticized landscapes; how many valleys were drowned, villagers dispossessed, in the passion for artificially-constructed lakes designed to look as though they were entirely the work of Nature in one of her finer moments?

No doubt climate has much to do with the emphasis on water in movement, and especially on fountains, in southern Europe – and in Persia and India too – as compared with chilly northern Europe, where there was little need to seek coolness even in summer. For all that, in Edwardian England, thanks to improvements in the science of hydraulics and the taste for things European, fountains became more popular in the gardens of the wealthy, or even of the comfortable middle classes.

Writing in *Gardens for Small Country Houses*, published in 1914, Gertrude Jekyll noted that in small gardens, 'little pools and rills and fountains, with their waters not too vigorously "jaillissantes", need to be disposed with a sparing hand'.

Even though Miss Jekyll's 'small' garden was, on the evidence of this and her other books, considerably more important than today's tiny plots, the principle holds good. And a simple wall fountain with a single jet, falling from a lion mask or a dolphin into a tiny pool, can be fitted into the smallest of spaces. After a succession of hot and droughty summers in formerly temperate Britain, shall we again see in our little gardens a resurgence on a small scale of fountains, fanciful masks spurting jets, and even splashing cascades, whose musicality is as soothing to the spirit as their cooling qualities are to the body dashed by the discomfort of heat?

ABOVE LEFT: Of Chatsworth's nine original fountains dating from the time of the first Duke, only one remains; the others were swept away by the fourth Duke, with Capability Brown's assistance. This charming, fantastical Willow Tree Fountain, a copper tree which sprays water in liquid mimicry of a weeping willow, is a reproduction of a fountain which may well have been created by Grillet, the pupil of the great French gardenmaker Le Nôtre, who designed the great cascade and fountains of the first Duke's Chatsworth.

LEFT: Barnsley House in the Cotswolds, has its water features too. The fine jets of the fountains cut through the leafy surround, composed of the bold leaves of hostas and *Ligularia clivorum*, the lime-green froth of lady's mantle, the jagged leaves of angelica and tree peonies. The fountain's design, by Simon Verity, recalls the economic importance of sheep in the Cotswold hills; the bas-relief of Purbeck stone, silhouetted against a backdrop of variegated ivy and rambling roses, shows two Cotswold rams. These are watered by the jets emerging from four Hornton stone frogs, carved by Judith Verity.

RIGHT: At Crathes Castle, Deeside, a garden of imagination verging on the eccentric, the single arching spray from the mouth of a tortoise carried on a cupid's back is echoed by the blooms of white buddleja, while in the foreground plumy white astilbes contrast with the clipped box surround and the horizontal lines of stone.

THE ROSE GARDEN

THERE IS HARDLY A
GARDEN IN ENGLAND THAT DOES NOT HAVE ITS ROSES.
THE ROSE, MORE THAN ANY OTHER BLOOM, IS AS MUCH
A SYMBOL AS A FLOWER. RED ROSES ARE SAID TO MEAN
'I LOVE YOU'. ENGLISH HISTORY HAS ITS WHITE ROSE OF
YORK AND RED ROSE OF LANCASTER WHICH GAVE THE
NAME TO THE WARS OF THE ROSES THAT ENDED WITH
THE VICTORY OF KING HENRY VII, THE FIRST TUDOR
MONARCH, IN 1485. IN CONTRAST TO THESE LOOSELY
DOUBLE ROSES, THE SCROLLED PERFECTION OF THE TEA
ROSES IS REDOLENT OF EDWARDIAN AFTERNOONS. IN
BETWEEN LIE THE OLD SHRUB ROSES WITH THEIR FLAT-
FACED, QUARTERED, GLOBULAR OR CUPPED BLOOMS. AT
WESTWELL MANOR, OXFORDSHIRE, THE GENEROUS
FLORAISON OF SHRUB ROSES IS SET IN THE SEMI-
FORMALITY OF BEDS SURROUNDED BY CLIPPED BOX
SPHERES, WITH PAVED PATHS BETWEEN THE BEDS.

Of all the roses we can grow, it is the old shrub roses and their rambling counterparts that speak most eloquently of the past; English history is full of them. Among the oldest of shrub roses are the Provence or cabbage roses so beloved of painters, which have been grown in European gardens for over two thousand years, well before the English ever existed, let alone thought of gardening; the alba roses to which belongs the white rose of York, emblem of the House of York in the civil strife known as the Wars of the Roses; the damask roses, which include among their number the rose known as the York and Lancaster rose (*Rosa* x *damascena versicolor*), for it bears both pink and white blooms on the same plant; the red rose of Lancaster itself, also known as the apothecary's rose (*Rosa gallica officinalis*), its intensely sweet-scented petals used to make confections and conserves as long ago as the thirteenth century, and Gerard's Old Velvet Rose, another gallica, dating from the sixteenth century. The striped gallica known affectionately as Rosa Mundi (*R. gallica* 'Versicolor'), though popular tradition associates it with the Fair Rosamund of England's King Henry II, is a sport of

ABOVE: At Haseley Court, Oxfordshire, featured on page 23 for its topiary, old roses, catmint and clary grow among apple trees, amid which is set this charming trellis confection with its bell-shaped superstructure topped with a little finial.

ABOVE: Foxgloves and sweet williams, favourite old-fashioned, cottage flowers, accompany shrub roses at The Menagerie, Northamptonshire. Not a single jarring note of the late twentieth century mars the peaceful, quintessentially English domestic landscape beyond the garden hedge.

LEFT: In a classic Sissinghurst combination, old roses – here 'Lavender Lassie', 'Prince Charles' and 'La Ville de Bruxelles' – grow with the star-spangled spheres of *Allium christophii* at their feet and a billowing white cloud of *Crambe cordifolia*, a relative of seakale, behind.

115

ABOVE: The tented arch of the trellis (seen left) is echoed, at Daylesford House, Gloucestershire, in the form of the pergola cross-members, not simple horizontals as is the norm, but of the same dipping, pointed arch outline, and painted in the same blue. Fragrant white 'Sanders' White Rambler' roses, in all their relaxed informality, point up the sharp angles and slender pillars.

LEFT: In the same garden, the climbing rose 'Alchymist' wreaths a trellis, its fragrant, soft yellow blooms, tinged with apricot and buff, is set off by the muted blue of the trellis and the seat it embowers and is echoed by the yellow single 'Golden Wings' in the foreground.

the apothecary's rose and may also date from no earlier than the sixteenth century (Rosamund herself died in 1176). The moss rose, so called because of the aromatic, mossy coat of green or brown covering the calyx and stem of the flower, appeared during the eighteenth century. In its pink form, it is immortalized in the 'Blind Earl' pattern of Worcester porcelain, in which the rosebuds decorating the borders of plates and dishes and saucers are raised in high relief, so that the sightless Earl of Coventry could still enjoy his beloved roses.

Many of the old roses that we grow today date from the nineteenth century, and were raised in France, as their names suggest: gallicas 'Belle de Crécy' in softest violet-mauve tinged with cerise, striped 'Camaieux', deep purple 'Cardinal Richelieu', albas 'Félicité Parmentier' and 'Madame Legras de St Germain', Provence roses 'Tour de Malakoff' and the curious crested moss, *Rosa centifolia* 'Cristata', dubbed 'Chapeau de Napoléon',

along with the true moss roses such as 'Blanche Moreau' and the sultry, maroon-purple 'Nuits de Young', and of course the Bourbons such as 'La Reine Victoria' and 'Madame Pierre Oger', 'Louise Odier', the opulent 'Madame Isaac Pereire' and the thornless, candy pink 'Zéphyrine Drouhin'. French they may be, but they are widely grown and loved in English gardens, where they are allowed more freedom than in France's formal, set-piece rose gardens. Even where, in an English garden, the frankly artificial confections of trellis and pergola, pillars and rope swags are decked with roses, there is always a sense of abandon compared with the rigorously-pruned French rose garden. The border at Hidcote (see page 122), though its roses are French, is entirely English, the plants allowed to grow into the shrubs that they truly are.

So these roses are of ancient ancestry, and their forebears were grown and loved, with passionate intensity, by Arabs and Persians and Mughals. In

ABOVE: Pink *Rosa* 'Bantry Bay' and crimson shrub roses are accompanied, at Ashtree Cottage, Wiltshire, by pale blue delphiniums (seen here after their main flowerheads have been cut down), purple catmint and viola, and white dusty miller (*Lychnis coronaria* 'Alba').

the time of the Abbasid caliphs, from the eighth to the thirteenth centuries, thirty thousand bottles of essence of red roses were sent each year from the rose distilleries of Bukhara to the caliph in Baghdad. To this day one can buy, for a few pence, garlands of intensely perfumed crimson roses in the cities of India and Pakistan, or a little bottle of attar of roses into which the very soul of the rose seems to have been distilled. It was no doubt in reference to these roses of the east and the south that Vita Sackville-West, finding among the nettles and brambles of Sissinghurst a surviving gallica rose with plum-purple blooms, named it 'Rose des Maures', though it is now known as 'Sissinghurst Castle', and its original name – if it ever had one – is probably lost for good. The Persian connection is acknowledged, too, in the damask rose 'Ispahan',

RIGHT: The original purpose of a pergola was to provide a walkway beneath the shade of vines, by way of protection from the hot meridional sun. In English gardens, as at Ashtree Cottage, the pergola becomes a way to display climbing and rambling roses, in default of or to supplement wall space or suitable host trees; shade is a secondary consideration. What is important, however, is to choose the appropriate roses for the pergola – shorter-growing, stiffer kinds are suitable for the uprights, perhaps, but for the cross-beams to be adequately clothed a rose of more relaxed habit is needed, and best of all one with flowers that nod, so that they can be enjoyed from below rather than wasting their beauty on the heedless skies. Here the white rose is 'Madame Butterfly' and the pink is 'Comte de Chambord'.

ABOVE: The careless abundance of 'Wedding Day', a white rambler, supported on crossing arches stands amid pink and crimson roses in a private garden. They are accompanied by a scattering of pink-eyed white lychnis and pure white foxgloves, whose tapering spires of nodding bells opening from alabaster-green buds are the perfect complement to the rounded outlines of both rose bush and rose bloom.

duced in 1792), 'Parson's Pink China' (1793) and lastly 'Park's Yellow Tea-Scented China' (1824) have come to be known as the four Stud Chinas, for it is their blood that has given us the high-centred, repeat- or perpetual-flowering tea roses and hybrid teas that represent another well-loved type of rose in many a garden.

In the latter part of the nineteenth century, when Dean Reynolds Hole was growing and showing roses, the hybrid perpetuals and tea roses were the novelties, supplanting the old shrub roses. They were grown as bushes and standards, with arches for climbing roses with supple stems and pillars for those of stiffer growth. The cupped or flat-faced bloom gave way to the high-centred flower opening from a scrolled bud, a form which was to reach its peak in the Hybrid Teas. But even Dean Hole, the moving spirit behind the National Rose Shows that remain so popular in England, also loved the old roses for garden use, however much he scorned them on the show bench.

The hybrid teas were show roses, bred for perfection of bloom, and the bush which bore those exquisite confections was a secondary consideration. In the cluster-flowered roses (or floribundas), it is the abundance of bloom rather than the form of each that matters; these are roses to make a splash of colour, which they do very effectively over a long season, though all too often without any accompanying fragrance. The old roses, and their modern cousins of the same style, on the other hand, are shrubs, and like other shrubs they lend themselves to growing with other plants that will complement their beauty. The best of English gardens, like the one at Sisinghurst (see page 115), makes full use of

while another damask, 'Omar Khayyam', was grown from seed brought from the grave of the mathematician-poet at Naishapur.

For centuries the burgeoning interest in plants for their own sakes, in northern Europe, was satisfied by introductions from the Mediterranean and the Near East, but in the nineteenth century, the heyday of the plant hunter, an amazing array of plants both wild and cultivated began to arrive from China and Japan. In 1809 a pink China rose was introduced to England, an old Chinese garden form which may already have been cultivated from as early as the sixteenth century in Italy. This, 'Hume's Blush Tea-Scented China', together with another three roses, 'Slater's Crimson China' (intro-

LEFT: In a private garden in Gloucestershire, a grand stone pillar, topped by a stone ball, and a white-painted gate echo the shell-pink rose 'New Dawn', a repeat-flowering rambler, that is flowering with such abandon alongside.

BELOW: A rustic bridge in a private garden in Shropshire, planted by Mirabel Osler, is embowered in *Rosa californica* 'Plena', a rose that flourishes in part-shade where the sun cannot fade its strong colour.

LEFT: In one of the garden rooms at Hidcote Manor, Gloucestershire, a long border is entirely given over to old French shrub roses. Vita Sackville-West, who greatly admired Hidcote, sought in her description of the garden to 'revive the memory of that June day and the loaded air, and the bushes weeping to the ground with the weight of their own bloom, a rumpus of colour, a drunkenness of scents'.

the English gift for combining plants. Not being confined in ghettos, they tend to be more resistant to disease than highly-bred modern roses (though some old roses are martyrs to black spot, it is true).

Old shrub roses are flattered by shrubs and perennials of domesticated appearance: mock orange (*Philadelphus*), cottage and Chinese peonies, double and cup-and-saucer forms of *Campanula persicifolia*, border pinks, with tulips to flower in spring amid the unfurling rose foliage, and border auriculas or violas as an edging or underplanting.

The old roses, almost without exception, bear flowers of gentle colouring, pale to rich pink often leaning towards mauve, crimson-reds (free of any hint of orange), magenta and soft grey-purple, and white which is more often tinged with blush or

ivory than stark white. Their flowers, and the bushes on which they are borne, are rounded in outline. The vertical notes of iris – supremely, *Iris pallida pallida* (also known as *I. pallida dalmatica*) with its broad, blue-grey sword leaves and blue fleur de lis flowers, but also the spurias in yellow or yellow-and-white – or of *Sisyrinchium striatum*, or of the crystalline white Madonna lily, contrast well in form. The deep maroon-crimson moss rose 'Nuits de Young' is enhanced by the primrose-buff bells of *Digitalis grandiflora*; white foxgloves are charming with pink roses, sophisticated among white ones. Contrariwise, companions that emphasize the notion of roundness may be chosen: the starry, metallic purple globes of *Allium christophii*, the domed heads of sweet williams. All the shades of

off-blue and lilac assort with old roses, purifying their pinkness: hardy geraniums such as 'Johnson's Blue' (equally lovely with yellow roses), bellflowers – especially *Campanula persicifolia* already mentioned, and also the tall *C. lactiflora* – larkspur, flowering sage; while alongside white flowers the richer-toned roses seem all the more vibrant.

Though some shrub roses have pleasant foliage – the rich green, ribbed leaves of *Rosa rugosa*, the grey-green of the alba roses, especially shell-pink 'Céleste' – their foliage is not, for the most part, notable. Companion plants such as *Alchemilla mollis*, hostas – especially the blue-leaved kinds – and the soft grey-purple *Salvia officinalis* 'Purpurascens', glaucous-leaved garden pinks, and all the silvers and greys, make good this deficiency.

What cannot be shown in illustrations is the fragrance that graces so many of these shrub roses. Though there is undoubtedly a kind of generic rose fragrance, instantly recognizable, each category of shrub rose that is endowed with scent, almost one might say each individual rose,

has its own characteristics. The vigorous ramblers with blood of the wild musk rose in them, almost all bearing large clusters of many small white flowers, have a generous, free-floating perfume with fruity components, apple or orange or banana. They can easily fill a whole garden with their perfume. The rugosas also waft their fragrance on the air, though it is quite different in quality, nearer to pure essence of rose without the fruity overtones. Without some likeness to a known fragrance to assist one's pen, it is impossible to convey in words even a hint of the nature of each type of rose fragrance; even so skilled a specialist as Graham Stuart Thomas, who knows his roses intimately and has great powers of description, admits as much and is forced back onto these words: 'Their fragrance is intense, intoxicating, and delicious. The scent of a sun-warmed Provence Rose, or a dew-cooled 'Maiden's Blush', is not surpassed for sweetness, although it may be equalled in its intensity, by flowers of any other genera.'

THE
CULINARY
GARDEN

THE EVENING LIGHT
AT HADSPEN GARDEN, SOMERSET, ILLUMINES A NEAT
VEGETABLE GARDEN WITH ITS BEAN ROWS AND RHUBARB
POTS, WHERE THE DECORATIVE QUALITIES OF
VEGETABLES ARE EXPLOITED TO THE FULL. THE BLUE-
GLAUCOUS BLADES OF LEEKS AND THE DEEP PURPLE
HEADS OF RED CABBAGE COMPLEMENT A LONG DRIFT OF
TALL VERBENA, ITS PURPLE FLOWERHEADS GLOWING
LIKE EMBERS IN THE LAST RAYS OF THE SUN, AND
RED-LEAVED LETTUCE GLANCES ACROSS THE PATH TO A
FLOWER BORDER ALL IN SHADES OF SCARLET,
CRIMSON AND MAHOGANY.

These days, when so much fresh produce, from all over the world, is available in supermarkets and greengrocers' shops, it is hard for us to imagine how monotonous must have been the daily diet in medieval Britain. There would have been game, fish on Fridays, and meat – fresh in summer, salted in winter – for the wealthy, and for the poor, such vegetables as they could grow (leeks, onions and garlic, curly kale, leaf beets and turnips) and fruit as they could collect in the hedgerows: wild raspberries, sharp little crab apples and the like. They might have enjoyed the occasional poached rabbit or fish, and would have had dried field-beans for winter protein. Yeoman farmers and the more prosperous cottagers would have had a pig and a few fowl in the yard, and beehives to ensure a supply of sweet honey.

Herbs were also grown, and used for many purposes: aromatics (a substitute for the costly spices from the east used by the aristocracy) to flavour pottage, or to mask the taste of salt meat that might be going off; a wide range of herbs for medicinal purposes; roses and other flowers and fruits for preserving and stilling; sweet herbs for strewing on the floor against lice, fleas and noxious smells. We know that by the early fifteenth century at least, the sweet

LEFT: Monasteries, in medieval times, had to be self-sufficient, not merely in produce, but also in herbs for strewing, to banish bad smells and insect pests, and for medicinal purposes. Many would have had walled gardens where their vegetables and herbs were grown. At Buckland Abbey, Devon, a herb garden in the style of a Tudor knot, with low box hedges separating herbs of different sorts. The variegated mint in the foreground, *Mentha suaveolens* 'Variegata', is edible but rather insipid, but the feathery purple fennel in the centre of the knot is just as aniseed-pungent as the green form, and far more decorative.

LEFT: The allotment style of vegetable gardening, with everything in long rows, is giving way to the French-inspired *potager*, which is both more decorative and more functional. Planting in short rows in blocks makes more effective use of a given space, and many varieties of vegetables are attractive to the eye as well as to the palate. In these box-edged beds in the kitchen garden at The Old Rectory, Sudborough, Northamptonshire, ruby and silver chard mingle around the base of a scarlet runner wigwam; there is no reason why beans should be grown in long rows either, however strong may be the hold on our imagination of W B Yeats' 'nine bean-rows' in his garden at Innisfree.

LEFT: There is no more reason to banish flowers from the vegetable garden than vice versa, and there is indeed a long tradition, in cottage and manorial gardens alike, of mingling the two. When the landscape designers of the eighteenth century decreed that mown grass should reach to the very foundations of the great houses of the time, it was in such productive gardens, out of sight of the fashion-conscious gentry, that the favourite old border flowers were preserved. At Barnsley House, Gloucestershire, the *potager* draws on twin traditions – the French and English – in which the notion of the landscaped *jardin anglais* was challenged by those who loved the fragrance and beauty of flowers.

or pungent aromatic shrubs of the Mediterranean – sage, hyssop, southernwood or lad's love (*Artemisia abrotanum*), and rue or herb of grace (*Ruta graveolens*) – were grown in England, soon to be followed by lavender and rosemary. Perhaps the English taste for pork with sage-and-onion stuffing and apple sauce dates from these times, the first joint of the newly-slaughtered pig eaten fresh while the rest was curing in brine to be eaten as ham or bacon later.

By the mid sixteenth century, we learn from Thomas Tusser's *A Hundred Good Points of Husbandry* that many different salad plants were grown in yeoman-farmers' gardens, for which the farmer's wife would have been responsible. Monasteries, manor houses and the great homes of the aristocracy would have had their walled gardens and orchards where vegetables and fruit were cultivated, the

ABOVE: Marrows and gourds are easily spoiled if grown flat on the ground; an arch from which they can hang is a decorative as well as a practical solution, adopted at Barnsley House. Tall sunflowers and ripening apples add to the sense of fecundity; soon it will be Keats' 'season of mists and mellow fruitfulness', but for the moment the glow of summer still holds this corner of the *potager* in its warmth.

ABOVE: Cornflowers and borage make a haze of blue, with the sunshine yellow of marigolds and the pink powder-puffs of opium poppies, in a small box-edged bed, with the bed beyond devoted to asparagus, now in its ferny stage, at Daylesford House, Gloucestershire. The narrow-topped, lidded pot is a rhubarb pot, used to force the tender young, pink shoots in spring; its simple, elegant and functional design make it handsome enough to be valued as a garden ornament too.

LEFT: Chives, savory, variegated mint, borage and lavender make an aromatic and softly colourful medley of herbs around borage and an imposing clump of teasels. In days gone by the spiky heads of teasels, once ripe and dried, were used by clothiers to tease up the nap of woollen cloth.

monks working their own land while the gentry and aristocracy had serfs, and later hired hands, to till the soil and raise the livestock and produce that kept the great houses going. Slowly the tradition developed of the head gardener presiding over a hierarchy of garden staff, some of them specialists with highly developed skills and knowledge in, say, the cultivation of vines or of pineapples under glass, down to the lowest form of life, the garden boy – who might, if he showed aptitude and enthusiasm, rise through the ranks to become, in turn, a head gardener tyrannizing the under-staff.

The country house was a centre of estate management and of domestic industry. A picture of the life in one such house, Claydon, Buckinghamshire seat of the Verneys, in the seventeenth century has

LEFT: Tall, clipped hedges make a tranquil enclave at York Gate, Yorkshire. In the still air the warmth of the sun brings out the spicy-sweet aromas of cotton lavender and rosemary, lavender and marjoram. The dominant visual theme is the circle or globe, whether in clipped golden privet, the flower- and seed-heads of alliums, or the central sundial. Box spirals and the paired yews clipped in ball-and-pillar style give an air of old-fashioned formality.

RIGHT: At Barnsley House, Gloucestershire, the lawnside herb garden, close to the former kitchen, forms a decorative pattern, with its interlacing hedges and the variety of culinary and aromatic plants that lodge in the squares and angles.

been preserved for us in the *Memoirs of the Verney Family*. The family was almost completely self-sufficient, with its own dairy, dovecotes and stew-pond, poultry and sheep and cattle and pigs, and 'apple and root chambers' for winter storage. There seem to have been few green vegetables and salads in the daily diet: if Thomas Tusser is to be believed, sixteenth-century yeoman farmers ate more, and more imaginative, salads than did the seventeenth-century gentry; indeed, it was not until after the Second World War that salads in England once again became as much appreciated as they had been in Shakespeare's day. No wonder the ladies of the Verney household and their female servants had to be skilled in preparing medicines from herbs according to the doctor's prescription or following the old family traditions; skin diseases and other ills of vitamin deficiency were very common. They also spun wool and flax, cooked, cured and preserved meats, distilled fragrant waters from lavender and rose petals, and made fruit syrups and home made wines from currants, cowslips and elder flowers and berries.

Though the aristocracy, shielded by landed wealth and supported by their dozens or even hundreds of domestic and estate servants, continued to live their lives almost unchanged in their great country estate, until the First World War overturned, for ever, the old certainties, there were tremendous social changes throughout Europe from the calamity of the Black Death onwards. So many people died of the Black Death in the fourteenth century that the surviving peasantry suddenly found themselves no longer serfs at the mercy of landlords, but able to negotiate a decent living wage because of the severe shortage of labour. By the sixteenth century, in Britain at least, political stability under the Tudors saw the emergence of a new middle class, many of whose members became enormously wealthy. The Industrial Revolution created another rich class, the new industrialists. The lives of many of the poor, too, were profoundly altered by the Industrial Revolution and the urbanization that accompanied it; those who moved to the industrial towns of the north in search of work no longer had anywhere to grow their own fruit and vegetables, and their diet, and no doubt their health, suffered as a result. By the late nineteenth century as we learn from Flora Thompson's *Lark Rise to Candleford*, farm wages were a pittance, and home-grown food was no luxury but an absolute necessity. 'The men took great pride in their gardens and allotments ... They ate plenty of green food, all home-grown and freshly-pulled'. For the farm labourer, then, the loss of common land was remedied to some extent by the provision of allotments and potato patches by philanthropic squires, parsons and farmers; but it was not until later that town-dwellers were to be offered allotments as of right, and it was never the case that everyone who wanted an allotment could be sure of being granted one.

In cottage gardens, at least as traditionally imagined, vegetables, fruit and flowers were all grown higgledy piggledy, with no attempt at segregation, though vegetables may have been grown in rows for ease of cultivation and harvesting. In much larger

LEFT: At The Old Rectory, Sudborough, Northampton-shire, low espaliered apples stand amid a plinth of lavender, with mint and the bold leaves of a marrow plant. Espaliered fruit trees grown on dwarfing stock make for an easy harvest, and can be fitted into a small space; they make an attractive and productive barrier between sections of the garden.

properties, where there was space for a separate kitchen garden, there would be long rows of each kind of vegetable, with a simple form of crop rotation practised; or, more typically in French and Swiss *jardins potagers*, blocks of short rows, intersected by narrow paths. There might be box-edged beds for herbs or a decorative edging of tiles around the vegetables. These *potagers* were not necessarily purely functional, and as much could be said of English kitchen gardens. In the domains that belonged to manor houses, there was often a walled garden where the beds of vegetables were separated by wide paths, along which there would be borders of hardy flowers, perhaps with espaliered apple trees, while on the walls grew the less hardy fruits:

ABOVE: An orchard tree on a non-dwarfing stock, allowed to grow freely, has a beauty of a different kind which compensates for the greater practical difficulties associated with pruning and picking. At Westwell Manor, Oxfordshire, a gnarled apple tree stands in a white foam of Queen Anne's lace. The phrase 'apple blossom' has come to symbolize the fresh-ness of spring, calling to mind the play of colours as crimson-pink buds open to pink-tinged flowers fading to pure white.

figs, peaches, nectarines and the like, that needed the extra warmth to ripen good, juicy fruit. Such a garden would be expected to yield not just the subsistence produce of the cottager, but luxury items as well, including pineapples from the hothouse and grapes from the vine house.

The best-known example of a *jardin potager* in the grand decorative style is in the reconstructed Renaissance gardens of Villandry, in the Loire region of France, which is laid out in box-edged squares, with trellis, vine-shaded pergolas and rose-wreathed arbours. Each of the squares is planted with a different variety of vegetable, chosen as much for their decorative qualities as their culinary value: blue-green cabbage, purple beet, the feathery bright green of carrot tops, golden maize among them. Villandry is a *potager* in the grand style; but the principles it enshrines could easily be translated to small plots, where their aesthetic qualities are immensely valuable; and a growing number of English gardeners are drawing inspiration from them. As can be seen at Barnsley

RIGHT: A band of chives in full mauve flower leads the eye onward, past a clump of golden marjoram, to the cascade of mauve that is *Buddleja alternifolia*, tucked into the corner where two walls meet, in this private Oxfordshire garden. One of the joys of planting culinary herbs among the flowers and shrubs of the garden, instead of in their own little ghetto herb garden, is that each expedition to snip a bouquet garni for the pot or a handful of fresh herbs for a salad becomes a tour of the garden, and the possibility of serendipitous encounters – a pansy or a nasturtium flower for the salad, perhaps, or a handful of petals of the rugosa rose 'Roseraie de l'Hay' to add perfume to a cup of Earl Grey tea.

ABOVE: At Tintinhull, Somerset, beds of vegetables are edged with catmint and decorated with mop-headed pillars of fragrant honeysuckle. Picking beans is no chore when the air is filled with perfume, and the best time is when the shadows are long, as now; for at dusk and dawn, honeysuckle is at its sweetest.

House (see page 130), no longer need the vegetable garden be purely utilitarian, a part of the garden to hide away behind a screen; it can be ornamental too.

Making the vegetable garden a thing of beauty in its own right is one way, where space permits. Another approach, better suited to more informally-designed gardens, is to bring the herbs, vegetables and fruit into the ornamental garden. Curly parsley, silver and ruby chard, red oak-leaf or fresh green salad bowl lettuce, scarlet runners and their pink- and white-flowered varieties, chives, rosemary, bay – which can be clipped into cones or spheres – are all worthy of a place in beds and borders among the flowers and ornamental foliage plants. As this list suggests, many herbs are decorative in leaf or flower or both, and several come in variegated or coloured-leaved form: purple-leaved, golden-variegated and tricolor sage as well as the traditional grey-green, golden marjoram, golden or gold-variegated balm, white-variegated apple mint and golden-striped ginger mint, are among the herbs that can join ornamental aromatics with silver or grey or glaucous foliage such as lavender, lad's love, cotton lavender (*Santolina*), curry plant (*Helichrysum italicum* – not for flavouring curries, but

named for its aroma of cheap curry powder) and pungent, glaucous blue rue.

Small wonder that today, despite the amazing diversity of vegetables and fruits available, often ready-washed and packaged, on supermarket shelves, many people still continue to grow their own produce on allotments or in their own back gardens; it may not make sense economically to do so any more, but the rewards lie elsewhere. Carrots no bigger than a child's finger, fresh-pulled from the soil as a row is thinned, and tossed over a hot flame in butter for a few minutes only; peas or baby broad beans raw from the pod; tiny new potatoes with the earth still clinging to them, scrubbed and boiled with a sprig of mint and accompanied by fresh-ground sea salt and butter; salad leaves crisp and sweet – none of these delights is to be had ready-packaged, and they are their own reward for the hard work that goes into producing them.

RUSTIC
CHARM

THIS HAMPSHIRE GARDEN

PRESENTS A CLASSIC IMAGE OF THE COTTAGE GARDEN:

A ROSE-EMBOWERED COTTAGE WITH DIAMOND-PANED

WINDOWS AMID A COLOURFUL MEDLEY OF FLOWERS.

PINK ROCK ROSES AND BLUE LOVE-IN-A-MIST, VIVID

MAGENTA-CRIMSON BYZANTINE GLADIOLUS OR CORN

FLAG, GOLDEN-LEAVED FEVERFEW, PURPLE CATMINT AND

WHITE DAISIES ARE AMONG THE FLOWERS THAT GROW

CHEEK BY JOWL IN THE BEDS AND BORDERS.

RIGHT: This picture, taken from the window of a cottage in Oxfordshire, almost guarantees to raise the spirits after the long, dark nights and chilly grey days of winter. All the favourites of spring are here: cottage tulips, forget-me-nots in classic azure blue and bridal white, polyanthus in colours as rich as ceremonial velvets.

ABOVE: Here is another face of cottage gardening: a mixture of regimented bright colours and rainbow mixtures in tubs, hanging baskets and window boxes. The long, low-built cottage with its grey slate roof and white walls that are such a flattering backdrop for the vivid flowers, snugly sheltering in the lee of the hillside, is typical of the north-western English region of Cumbria. The rainfall is high in these regions, the skies more often grey than cloudless; an abundance of warm colours, red and yellow, is more than ever welcome.

When the French talk of *le jardin anglais*, they mean the great idealized landscapes of the eighteenth century, or at least a kind of mental pastiche of this style, so different, in its smooth lawns, rolling contours and carefully placed clumps of trees, from the static formality of great French gardens. If there is one style that is now 'typically' English, however, it is a romanticized version of the cottage garden, deriving from twin strands: on the one hand the utilitarian gardening of the true cottager, where flowers were appreciated but had to take second place to vegetables, fruit and herbs, and on the other the gentrified cottage garden of the Picturesque movement, which consciously looked back to an idyllic past that never was. An appreciation of heritage at the expense of creative innovation is no new thing.

Even such sophisticated twentieth-century gardens as Hidcote and Sissinghurst, undoubtedly the work of creative innovators, and inspiration for countless gardeners the world over who have visited these hallowed sites or even merely read about them – even they draw on a particular perception of the cottage-garden style for their planting, if not for their design. This style endures at least in part because it answers so well a particular impulse of gardeners in Britain, fostered by the climate: the urge to grow a great variety of plants from many different regions of the world, an urge which some times subsumes the impulse to good design.

Cottage gardens, indeed, are hardly designed, in the true sense of the word; the basic enclosure with its path from gate to cottage door imposes a kind of order, but no more.

Intimate, profusely planted, flowery, colourful, fragrant with roses and honeysuckle, a 'sweet confusion of the useful and the ornamental', as Edward

LEFT: In *Lark Rise to Candleford*, Flora Thompson wrote of the corner of the cottage garden that was given up to flowers, 'not growing in beds or borders, but crammed together in an irregular square, where they bloomed in half-wild profusion'. Those words could have been written of this very garden in Steeple Aston, Oxfordshire, where bellflowers and scarlet Maltese cross (*Lychnis chalcedonica*), yellow loosestrife and pink and white roses are jumbled together with not a space for a weed to intrude.

Hyams described it: such is the image of the cottage garden. Before the influx of exotic plants that now seem so much at home in English cottage gardens, plants that we might now think of as ornamental were included more for their utility than their beauty: apothecary's rose, lily-of-the-valley, Solomon's seal, stinking hellebore, greater celandine, soapwort (so-called because it makes a cleansing lather), broom, meadowsweet – this last with many virtues, from medicinal to its value as a sweet strewing herb and its use to flavour mead, a drink made from fermented honey. With space for a few orchard trees, there might be a bullace-plum (*Prunus insititia*), a medlar, a crab apple. And for their magical, protective qualities, there might well be a yew or a rowan.

RIGHT: Addisford Cottage, in Devon, is typical of the region, with its whitewashed cob walls, little porch in which to shelter from the sou'westerly gales, and thatched roof. The plants that grow in its garden include some of the oldest cottage favourites: the apothecary's rose (*Rosa gallica officinalis*), the old tawny daylily (*Hemerocallis fulva*), irises, and, of course, the ubiquitous foxglove, a native plant that has staked a claim in almost every garden in the land.

ABOVE: There is something irresistibly innocent about a white daisy, to say nothing of the pink pyrethrums alongside them. Both are classic early summer border flowers that coincide in their season, as in this Gloucestershire garden, with lupins and foxgloves.

LEFT: Foxgloves have the knack of placing themselves where they most flatter their neighbours; or perhaps this planting, in an Oxfordshire garden, is the result of that particular skill which resides in making the studied seem natural. The thatched roof, gothick window and wooden paling fence make a timeless picture with the spires of the foxglove and the tousled 'Albertine' rose on the wall.

BELOW: The satin finish of these mallow flowers (*Malope trifida*), and the narrow slits at the base through which the green calyx gleams in contrast to the vivid rosy red petals, make this a favourite summer annual for those who love to observe the detail of their flowers. The malope is growing, along with white double shasta daisies, pale pink *Lavatera* 'Silver Cup', pink and blue cornflowers and yellow anthemis, in a Dorset garden, in a typical glad, artless jumble.

Forms of native flowers chosen for their curiosity might also find a home in cottage plots amid the onions and kale: white and pink violets as well as the more usual blue, the double yellow buttercup known as bachelor's buttons, white or pink foxgloves, primroses and polyanthus in unusual colours or with double or green-ruffed flowers, known as jack-in-the-green, or – evoking fashionable male legwear of Elizabethan England – hose-in-hose, in which the primrose is formed of not one but two corollas, one within the other. There were a few exotics too. Among very early introductions that we now regard as cottage garden plants are the Madonna lily (*Lilium candidum*), which was brought to Britain by the Romans; cottage peonies (*Paeonia officinalis*) with crimson, pink or white flowers, the first introduction of which predates the Norman Conquest; wallflowers; the vivid scarlet Maltese cross or Jerusalem cross (*Lychnis chalcedonica*), its presence in English gardens dating from the time of the

OVERLEAF: Gloucestershire's houses and cottages are built of the local Cotswold stone, which is often of a soft creamy-grey tint, the perfect complement to this vivid spring scene where grape hyacinths are echoed, across the daisy-spangled lawn, by the paler azure of forget-me-nots, with polyanthus in a dozen jewel colours scattered between, and scarlet tulips arising grenadier-like from amidst the medley.

147

RIGHT: In the garden of Addisford Cottage, Devon, the soft, cloudy outlines of cranesbills are half hidden among spires and swords – steepling foxgloves in purple and white, the pleated blade leaves of crocosmias and the spears of irises, and the narrow spikes of *Sisyrinchium striatum*, its little straw yellow flowers, daintily veined with purple on the reverse, hugging the narrow stems.

LEFT: Hollyhocks have been grown in England's cottage gardens for centuries; both Gerard, in his famous *Herball* of 1597, and Thomas Tusser, who wrote *A Hundred Good Points of Husbandry* of 1557 in verse for the edification of tenant farmers and their wives, mention them. The butterfly bush (*Buddleja davidii*), on the other hand, is quite a newcomer, introduced from China only about one hundred years ago. Against the backdrop of a honey-coloured stone and thatched cottage in Warwickshire, the pink and pastel trumpets of the hollyhocks set off the vibrant purple tassels of the butterfly bush.

ladder (*Polemonium caeruleum*), the peach-leaved bellflower (*Campanula persicifolia*) and chimney bellflower (*C. pyramidalis*), the trailing perennial peas with their magenta, pink or white flowers, the cardinal flower (*Lobelia cardinalis*), and the double white fair maids of France (*Ranunculus aconitifolius* 'Flore Pleno') – and the list could be much longer. From the kitchen gardens of the great houses some of them found their way, as seeds or slips, to the humbler gardens of cottagers, who, heedless of high fashion, loved them for their beauty and their fragrance. Thus it was that the old flowers were preserved, to be rediscovered when fashion again changed in their favour.

These cottage gardens were lovingly described by the poet John Clare (1793–1864), the son of a poor labourer who began his working life tending sheep and geese on the village common in his native Northamptonshire, and who wrote of the rustic life that was all he knew. He extolled a 'little garden not too fine, enclosed with painted pales', and he described the flowers that cottagers loved to grow there,

> ... the best flowers, not those of wood and fields,
> But such as every farmer's garden yields –
> Fine cabbage roses, painted like her face,
> The shining pansy, trimm'd with golden lace,
> The tall-topped larkheels, feather'd thick with flowers,
> The woodbine, climbing o'er the door in bowers,
> The London tufts, of many a mottled hue,
> The pale pink pea, and monkshood darkly blue,
> The white and purple gilliflowers, that stay
> Ling'ring, in blossom, summer half away,
> The single blood-walls, of a luscious smell,
> Old-fashion'd flowers which housewives love so well,
> The columbines, stone-blue, or deep night-brown,
> Their honeycomb-like blossoms hanging down
> Each cottage-garden's fond adopted child,
> Though heaths still claim them, where they yet grow
> wild.

This image of the cottage garden was perpetuated by the watercolour paintings of Helen Allingham (1846–1926), who wanted to capture what the old cottages and their gardens looked like before they disappeared for good; and by the account of cottage life during an Oxfordshire

Crusades; and clove pinks or clove gilliflowers, the ancestor of which came with the Normans. With their strong, sweet scent of cloves, they were used to add flavour to the cloudy ale which was the usual beverage of the English labourer, and even to wine – one variety is called sops-in-wine.

When, in the eighteenth century, flower gardens were banished from the domains of England's great houses, these and other favourite old flowers were relegated, along with the old aromatics of the Mediterranean, to the kitchen garden. Among them were such stalwarts of today's flower gardens as oriental poppies, monkshoods, tulips (for which whole fortunes had been lost, in the seventeenth century), crown imperials (*Fritillaria imperialis*), hollyhocks, globe thistles, *Delphinium elatum*, mountain knapweed (*Centaurea montana*) with its blue cornflowers, yellow *Anthemis tinctoria*, St Bernard's and St Bruno's lilies (*Anthericum liliago* and *Paradisea liliastrum*), the old tawny daylily (*Hemerocallis fulva*) and the fragrant lemon lily (*H. lilio-asphodelus*), columbines, goat's rue (*Galega species*), the old purple bearded iris, bergamot (*Monarda fistulosa*), Jacob's

childhood in the 1880s in Flora Thompson's trilogy *Lark Rise to Candleford*. Nostalgically, she described the flower garden of an elderly couple who, unlike the younger agricultural workers on bare subsistence wages, had lived their working lives at a time when there was relative prosperity in rural areas. In the old couple's garden 'Sally had such flowers, and so many of them, and nearly all of them sweet-scented! Wallflowers and tulips, lavender and sweet-william, and pinks, and old world roses with enchanting names – Seven Sisters, Maiden's Blush, moss rose, monthly rose, cabbage rose, blood rose and most thrilling of all to the children, the big bush of the York and Lancaster rose'.

No wonder Miss Jekyll could write: 'I have learned much from the little cottage gardens that help to make our English waysides the prettiest in the temperate world'. And as these cottages that

ABOVE: Smocking may not be fashionable these days, but for a scarecrow what could be more appropriate? After all, a scarecrow is himself unfashionable now that there is all that glitter and bang available to keep the birds off the crops; so he might as well wear the white smock and red kerchief of centuries past, as he keeps watch over hostas and globe flowers, angelica, fennel and purle-leaved brassica. He stands in Wilderness Farm, in Sussex.

RIGHT: The cottages of Britain are very diverse; for unlike great houses, they would be made from the local materials, stone or cob or brick or, as here in Kent, from wooden clapboarding, painted white, beneath a tiled roof. The narrow path, leading straight from the gate to the cottage door, is typical, and the casual profusion of roses, poppies and shasta daisies, with more roses on the house walls, is a happy twentieth-century interpretation of the old, artless cottage style of planting.

were once, even as late as the 1960s, inhabited by farm and estate workers and gardeners employed by the local lord of the manor, have become homes with modernized, *tout-confort* interiors for city workers, so the gardens that surround them have been consciously prettified, planted with the sweet old-fashioned flowers and more recent exotics alike. Having spent so long in exile, as it were, from the gardens of the nobility and the gentry (for in

geese, and thus it was that almost every cottage had a simple gate, wooden or wrought iron, opening from the dusty road onto a narrow path leading straight to the cottage door. Hedges were often trimmed neatly into arches or pillars framing the garden gate, in keeping with the cottagers' taste for simple topiary. In the case of houses belonging to yeoman farmers, where a farmyard might directly adjoin the fields, there would be a farm gate, wider

RIGHT: It was the tradition to plant a yew tree near the cottage, to keep away both the wind and the evil spirits that might be lurking there. This crested bird-cum-arch in a Herefordshire garden could hardly keep the wind at bay, but cottage topiary of such light-hearted nature would surely banish the most malevolent of spirits.

ABOVE: In Derbyshire, a wooden gate, rather lopsided, lit by the sun; a green arch; and a depth of black shadow that conceals who knows what? A rustic Sleeping Beauty? A secret garden? The imagination, unfettered, might create a whole fantasy around this simple country scene.

Victorian times, it was exotic bedding plants, not hardy perennials, that captured the imaginations of the fashionable and those who aped them), these hardy flowers now belong as much to the cottage gardens where they survived the decades of neglect as they do to the grander or more sophisticated borders of Chapter 4.

Unlike the unfenced front gardens common in North America, Britain's cottage gardens have always tended to be enclosed by a fence or wall or hedge, for the practical reason that they were surrounded by open, strip-farmed fields in medieval times; and even after these had been transformed into the now familiar patchwork of hedged or walled fields, there remained in most villages an open common where peasants could pasture their beasts. Some kind of barrier was essential to protect the precious garden crops from straying cattle or

than the front gate, separating the yard from the fields, for cattle to be brought into the byre or the haycart into the barn. In the days before mechanical trimmers that lay waste all before them, farm hedges of thorn or beech or a mixture of species would be cut-and-laid, and promising young saplings would be spared and encouraged to grow into straight, strong trees, to provide shade and shelter for livestock.

Over the centuries, changing patterns of agriculture and the enduring appeal of cottages, the artless gardens that surround them, and the flowers and shrubs and herbs that fill them with colour and fragrance, have formed the face of the English countryside with its fields and hedgerows, the English village with its houses and cottages built of local materials, and lastly the idealized cottage garden as we know it today.

RIGHT: The transition from garden to surrounding meadow is beautifully handled at Vann, Surrey, by the simple expedient of setting, either side of the five-barred farm gate, a pair of beeches rising from the hedge of which they are part, and clipped into domes. All the nostalgia of autumn is in this scene: the warm colours, the crisp chill in the air, and the half pleasurable, half fearful anticipation of winter to come.

GARDENS TO VISIT

The following gardens are open to the public. Opening arrangements, for these and other notable gardens, are given in *The Good Gardens Guide* (ed. G. Rose and P. King), published annually by Vermilion Books, London.
Tel: 0171 9739690

ARLEY HALL
Near Northwich
Cheshire CW9 6NA
Tel: 01565 777353

ADDISFORD COTTAGE
West Lane
Dolton
Devon EX19 8QU
Tel: 01805 804365

BARNSLEY HOUSE
GARDEN
Barnsley
Gloucestershire GL7 4EE
Tel: 01285 740281

BRAMDEAN HOUSE
Bramdean
Alresford
Hampshire SO24 0JU
Tel: 01962 771214

BROUGHTON CASTLE
Banbury
Oxfordshire OX15 5EB
Tel: 01295 262624

BUCKLAND ABBEY
Yelverton
Devon PL20 6EY
Tel: 01822 853607

CHATSWORTH
Bakewell
Derbyshire DE45 1PP
Tel: 01246 582204

CHENIES MANOR HOUSE
Chenies
Buckinghamshire
WD3 6ER
Tel: 01494 762888

CRATHES CASTLE
Banchory
Kincardine and Deeside
AB31 3QJ
Tel: 01330 844525

THE GARDEN HOUSE
Buckland Monachorum
Yelverton
Devon PL10 7LQ
Tel: 01822 854769

HADDON HALL
Bakewell
Derbyshire DE45 1LA
Tel: 01629 812855

HADSPEN GARDEN
Castle Cary
Somerset BA7 7NG
Tel: 01963 50939

HERTERTON HOUSE
Cambo, Morpeth
Northumberland
NE61 4BN
Tel: 01670 774278

HESTERCOMBE HOUSE
GARDENS
Cheddon Fitzpaine
Somerset TA2 8LQ
Tel: 01823 337222

HIDCOTE MANOR
GARDENS
Chipping Campden
Gloucestershire GL55 6LR
Tel: 01386 438333

HOUSE OF PITMUIES
Guthrie
By Forfar
Angus DD8 2SN
Tel: 01241 828245

KIFTSGATE COURT
GARDEN
Chipping Campden
Gloucestershire
GL55 6LW
Tel: 01386 438777

KNIGHTSHAYES COURT
Bolton
Tiverton
Devon EX16 7RQ
Tel: 01884 254665

LEVENS HALL
Kendal
Cumbria LA8 0PD
Tel: 015395 60321

LITTLE THAKEHAM
Merrywood Lane
Storrington
West Sussex RH20 3HE
Tel: 01903 744416

THE LOST GARDENS OF
HELIGAN
Pentewan
St Austell
Cornwall PL26 6EN
Tel: 01726 844157

MAGDALEN COLLEGE
Oxford
Oxfordshire
Tel: (Bursar's office) 01865 276050

THE MENAGERIE
Horton
Northamptonshire
NN7 2BX
Tel: 01536 418205

THE OLD RECTORY
Sudborough
Near Kettering
Northamptonshire
NN14 3BX
Tel: 01832 733247

POWIS CASTLE
Welshpool
Powys SY21 8RF
Tel: 01938 554336

THE PRIORY
Kemerton
Near Tewkesbury
Hereford and Worcester
GL20 7JN
Tel: 01386 725258

ROYAL BOTANIC
GARDENS, KEW
Richmond
Surrey TW9 3AB
Tel: 0181 9401171

ROYAL HORTICULTURAL
SOCIETY GARDEN,
ROSEMOOR
Great Torrington
Devon EX38 8PH
Tel: 01805 624067

SALING HALL
Great Saling
Braintree
Esex CM7 5DT
Tel: 01371 850243

SISSINGHURST CASTLE
GARDEN
Cranbrooke
Kent TN17 2AB
Tel: 01580 712850

STICKY WICKET
Buckland Newton
Dorset DT2 7BY
Tel: 01300 345476

STOBO WATER GARDEN
Stobo
Near Peebles
Tweeddale
Tel: 01721 760216

STONE LANE GARDENS
Stone Farm
Chagford
Devon
Tel: 01647 231311

STOURHEAD
Stourton
Warminster
Wiltshire
BA12 6QD
Tel: 01747 841152

STOWE LANDSCAPE
GARDENS
Near Buckingham
Buckinghamshire
MK18 5EH
Tel: 01280 822850

TINTINHULL HOUSE
GARDEN
Farm Street
Tintinhull
Near Yeovil
Somerset
BA22 9PZ
Tel: 01935 822545

VANN
Hambledon
Surrey GU8 4EF
Tel: 01428 683413

WALLINGTON
Cambo
Morpeth
Northumberland
NE61 4AR
Tel: 01670 774283

WATERPERRY GARDENS
Wheatley
Oxfordshire OX33 1JL
Tel: 01844 339254/266

WILDERNESS FARM
Hadlow Down
Sussex TN22 4HU
Tel: 01825 830552

The following gardens are
open on certain days each
year, and sometimes by
special appointment.
Opening times and further
details are listed in *Gardens
Open for Charity* published
annually by
The National Gardens
Scheme
Hatchlands Park
East Clandon
Guildford
Surrey GU4 7RT
Tel: 01483 211535

23 BEECHCROFT ROAD
Summertown
Oxford
Oxfordshire

COURT HOUSE
East Quantoxhead
Somerset

DAYLESFORD HOUSE
Daylesford
Oxfordshire

FARINGDON HOUSE
Faringdon
Oxfordshire

FRITH LODGE
Northchapel
Sussex

GARSINGTON MANOR
Garsington
Oxfordshire

HASELY COURT
Little Haseley
Oxfordshire

PENNS IN THE ROCKS
Groombridge
Sussex

STOBSHIEL
Humbie
East Lothian

WESTWELL MANOR
Westwell
Near Burford
Oxfordshire

YORK GATE
Back Church Lane
Adel
Leeds
Yorkshire

INDEX